THE GOLDEN JOURNEY

The Golden Journey

POEMS FOR YOUNG PEOPLE

compiled by LOUISE BOGAN
and WILLIAM JAY SMITH

woodcuts by FRITZ KREDEL

Henry Regnery Company
Chicago

Copyright © 1965 by Louise Bogan and William Jay Smith
All rights reserved, including the right to reproduce this book
or portions therein in any form.
Published by Henry Regnery Company
180 North Michigan Avenue, Chicago, Illinois 60601
Manufactured in the United States of America
Library of Congress Catalog Card Number: 65-21489
International Standard Book Number: 0-8092-8689-0 (cloth)
0-8092-7963-0 (paper)

COPYRIGHT ACKNOWLEDGMENTS

The compilers of THE GOLDEN JOURNEY and the Henry Regnery Company wish to thank the following authors, publishers, and agents for permission to reprint copyrighted material. Every possible effort has been made to trace the ownership of each poem included. If any errors or omissions have occurred, correction will be made in subsequent editions, provided that the publisher is notified of their existence.

GEORGE ALLEN & UNWIN, LTD. for "The Hammers" by Ralph Hodgson from *Collected Poems*. Reprinted by permission of George Allen & Unwin, Ltd.
APPLETON-CENTURY (an affiliate of Meredith Press) for "The Flower-Fed Buffaloes" by Vachel Lindsay from *Going to the Stars* by Vachel Lindsay, copyright, 1926, by D. Appleton & Company. Reprinted by permission of Appleton-Century.
MRS. GEORGE BAMBRIDGE, MACMILLAN & CO., LTD. and **THE MACMILLAN CO. OF CANADA, LTD.**, for "Cities and Thrones and Powers" from *Puck of Pook's Hill* by Rudyard Kipling, copyright, 1906, by Rudyard Kipling. Reprinted by permission of Mrs. George Bambridge, Macmillan & Co., Ltd. and The Macmillan Co. of Canada, Ltd.
EDMUND BLUNDEN for "The Midnight Skaters."
THE BODLEY HEAD, LTD. for "There'd be an Orchestra" from the poem "Thousand-and-First Ship" from *The Crack-Up* by F. Scott Fitzgerald, from *The Bodley Head Scott Fitzgerald*, Vol. III and for "The Too-Late Born" by Archibald MacLeish from *Poems* by Archibald MacLeish. Reprinted by permission of The Bodley Head, Ltd.
BRANDT & BRANDT for "Portrait of a Girl" from "Priapus and the Pool" by Conrad Aiken from *Collected Poems of Conrad Aiken*, copyright by Conrad Aiken. Reprinted by permission of Brandt & Brandt.
JONATHAN CAPE, LTD. for "Naming of Parts" by Henry Reed, and for "Alba" by Derek Walcott. These poems reprinted by permission of Jonathan Cape, Ltd.
THE CLARENDON PRESS for "I Have Loved Flowers" by Robert Bridges from *The Shorter Poems of Robert Bridges*. Reprinted by permission of The Clarendon Press.
MISS D. E. COLLINS and **METHUEN & CO., LTD.** for "The Song of Quoodle" by G. K. Chesterton from *The Flying Inn* by G. K. Chesterton. Reprinted by permission of Miss D. E. Collins and Methuen & Co., Ltd.

FRANK COLLYMORE for "The Zobo Bird."
PADRAIC COLUM for "I Saw the Wind Today."
THE CRESSET PRESS for "To a Fat Lady Seen from a Train" by Frances Cornford.
CURTIS BROWN, LTD. for the two poems by Kenneth Grahame from *The Wind in the Willows* by Kenneth Grahame, and for the selections by William Jay Smith; Curtis Brown, Ltd. and X. J. Kennedy for "Little Elegy" by X. J. Kennedy, copyright, ©, 1960, by X. J. Kennedy. Reprinted by permission of X. J. Kennedy.
THE JOHN DAY COMPANY, INC. for "Fife Tune" by John Manifold from *Selected Verse* by John Manifold, copyright, 1946, by The John Day Company.
J. M. DENT & SONS, LTD. for "The Purist" by Ogden Nash from *Family Reunion* by Ogden Nash; and for "Fern Hill" by Dylan Thomas from *Collected Poems* by Dylan Thomas and "Johnnie Crack and Flossie Snail" by Dylan Thomas from *Under Milk Wood* by Dylan Thomas. All these poems reprinted by permission of J. M. Dent & Sons, Ltd.
THE DEVIN-ADAIR COMPANY for "Condors" by Padraic Colum from *The Collected Poems of Padraic Colum*, published 1954, by The Devin-Adair Company. Reprinted by permission of the publishers.
DODD, MEAD & COMPANY, INC. for "The Song of Quoodle" by G. K. Chesterton from *The Collected Poems of G. K. Chesterton*, copyright, 1932, by Dodd, Mead & Company, Inc.
DOUBLEDAY & COMPANY, INC. for "Little Elegy," copyright, ©, 1960, by X. J. Kennedy from *Nude Descending a Staircase* by X. J. Kennedy; and for "The Bat" by Theodore Roethke, copyright, 1938, 1939, by Theodore Roethke, "The Lady and the Bear" by Theodore Roethke, copyright, 1951, by Theodore Roethke, "The Big Wind" by Theodore Roethke, copyright, 1947, by The United Chapters of Phi Beta Kappa, all from *Words for the Wind* by Theodore Roethke, all these poems reprinted by permission of Doubleday & Company, Inc.; and for "Cities and Thrones and Powers" by Rudyard Kipling from *Rudyard Kipling's Verse: Definitive Edition*, reprinted by permission of Mrs. George Bambridge and Doubleday & Company, Inc.
E. P. DUTTON & COMPANY, INC. for "The Wind and the Moon" by George Macdonald from *Poems* by George Macdonald and for "The Three Foxes" by A. A. Milne from the book *When We Were Very Young* by A. A. Milne, copyright, 1924, by E. P. Dutton & Co., Inc., renewal, 1952, by A. A. Milne. These poems reprinted by permission of the publishers.
NORMA MILLAY ELLIS for "Counting-Out Rhyme" and "Look, Edwin!" by Edna St. Vincent Millay from *Collected Poems*, Harper & Row, copyright, 1929, 1956, by Edna St. Vincent Millay and Norma Millay Ellis.
FABER & FABER, LTD. for "Their Lonely Betters" by W. H. Auden from *Nones* by W. H. Auden; for "Cape Ann" by T. S. Eliot from *Collected Poems 1909–62* by T. S. Eliot, copyright, 1963, by T. S. Eliot; for "The Express" by Stephen Spender from *Collected Poems* by Stephen Spender; for the three poems by Wallace Stevens from *The Collected Poems of Wallace Stevens;* for "Digging for China" by Richard Wilbur from *Poems 1943–56* by Richard Wilbur. All these poems reprinted by permission of Faber & Faber, Ltd.
FARRAR, STRAUS & GIROUX, INC. and PETER OWEN, LTD. for the two poems by Louise Bogan from *Collected Poems 1923–1958*, copyright, 1958, by Louise Bogan. Reprinted by permission of the publishers.

v

FUNK & WAGNALLS for "Country Summer" and "Song from a Country Fair" by Léonie Adams from *Poems: A Selection* by Léonie Adams, copyright, 1954, by Léonie Adams. Reprinted by permission of Funk & Wagnalls.

GROVE PRESS, INC. for "Oread" by H. D. from *H. D. Selected Poems*, copyright, 1957, by Norman Holmes Pearson. Reprinted by permission of Grove Press, Inc.

HARCOURT, BRACE & WORLD, INC. for "All in Green Went My Love Riding" by E. E. Cummings from *Poems 1923–1954* by E. E. Cummings, copyright, 1923, 1951, by E. E. Cummings; for "Cape Ann" by T. S. Eliot from *Collected Poems 1909–1962* by T. S. Eliot, copyright, 1936, by Harcourt, Brace & World, Inc., ©, 1963, 1964, by T. S. Eliot; for "Naming of Parts" by Henry Reed from *A Map of Verona and Other Poems* by Henry Reed, copyright, 1947, by Henry Reed; for "At the Bottom of the Well" by Louis Untermeyer from *Long Feud* by Louis Untermeyer, copyright, 1928, by Harcourt, Brace & World, Inc., renewed ©, 1956, by Louis Untermeyer; for 'Digging for China" by Richard Wilbur from *Things of This World*, ©, 1956, by Richard Wilbur. All these poems reprinted by permission of Harcourt, Brace & World, Inc.

RUPERT HART-DAVIS, LTD. and ANDREW YOUNG for "The Old Tree" and "Daisies" by Andrew Young from *The Collected Poems of Andrew Young*. Reprinted by permission of Rupert Hart-Davis, Ltd. and Andrew Young. Rupert Hart-Davis, Ltd. and Charles Causley for "Nursery Rhyme of Innocence and Experience" by Charles Causley. Reprinted by permission of Rupert Hart-Davis, Ltd. and Charles Causley.

HARVARD UNIVERSITY PRESS for "Cold Are the Crabs" and the quatrains by Edward Lear from *Teapots and Quails and Other New Nonsense* by Edward Lear, edited by Angus Davidson and Philip Hofer, copyright, 1953, by the President and Fellows of Harvard College. Reprinted by permission of Harvard University Press.

HOLT, RINEHART & WINSTON, INC. for the selections from *Complete Poems of Robert Frost*, copyright, 1916, 1921, 1923, 1930, 1934, 1939, by Holt, Rinehart & Winston, Inc., copyright, 1944, 1951, ©, 1958, 1962, by Robert Frost; for "Into My Heart" from *A Shropshire Lad*—authorized edition—from *The Collected Poems of A. E. Housman*, copyright, 1940, by Holt, Rinehart & Winston, Inc.; and for "Lydia is Gone This Many a Year" from *The Selected Poems of Lizette Woodworth Reese*, copyright, 1926, by Holt, Rinehart & Winston, Inc., copyright, 1954, by C. Reese Dietrich. All these poems reprinted by permission of Holt, Rinehart & Winston, Inc.

HORNRO N. V. AND INTERNATIONAL AUTHORS N. V. for the selections by Robert Graves from *Robert Graves' Collected Poems*, copyright, 1956, 1959, 1960, by International Authors N. V. Reprinted by permission of Hornro N. V. and International Authors N. V.

HOUGHTON MIFFLIN COMPANY for "Grizzly Bear" by Mary Austin, "The Fish" by Elizabeth Bishop, "First Song" by Galway Kinnell, "The Too-Late Born" by Archibald MacLeish from *Collected Poems*, copyright, 1952, by Archibald MacLeish. All reprinted by permission of Houghton Mifflin Company.

MISS BARBARA HOWES for "Landscape: Deer Season."

INDIANA UNIVERSITY PRESS for "Dahlias" from *The Vegetable Kingdom* by Padraic Colum, copyright, 1954, by Indiana University Press. Reprinted by permission of Indiana University Press.

ALFRED A. KNOPF, INC. for "Sarah Byng" and "The Frog" by Hilaire Belloc, copyright, 1931, by Hilaire Belloc, renewed, 1959, by Eleanor Jebb Belloc,

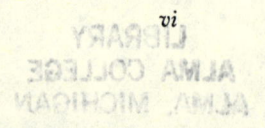

Elizabeth Belloc, and Hilary Belloc, reprinted from *Cautionary Verses* by Hilaire Belloc; for "Velvet Shoes," copyright, 1921, by Alfred A. Knopf, Inc., renewed 1949, by William Rose Benét, reprinted from *Collected Poems of Elinor Wylie;* and for the three poems by Wallace Stevens, copyright, 1923, and renewed 1951, by Wallace Stevens, reprinted from *Collected Poems of Wallace Stevens*. All these poems reprinted by permission of Alfred A. Knopf, Inc.

LITTLE, BROWN & COMPANY for the selections by Emily Dickinson from *The Complete Poems of Emily Dickinson;* for "Tiger Lily" from *Far and Few* by David McCord, copyright, 1939, by David McCord; for "The Purist" from *Verses from 1929 On* by Ogden Nash, copyright, 1935, by The Curtis Publishing Company; for "Eletelephony" from *Tirra Lirra* by Laura E. Richards, copyright, 1935, by Laura E. Richards; for "Dog" and "Butterfly" by William Jay Smith from *Boy Blue's Book of Beasts* by William Jay Smith, copyright, 1956, 1957, by William Jay Smith, and for "A Pavane for the Nursery" from *Poems 1947–1957* by William Jay Smith, copyright, 1954, by William Jay Smith. All these poems included by permission of Little, Brown & Company.

MRS. HUGH LOFTING and JONATHAN CAPE, LTD. for "Picnic" by Hugh Lofting from *Porridge Poetry* by Hugh Lofting, copyright, 1924, 1953. Reprinted by permission of Mrs. Lofting and the publishers.

MACGIBBON & KEE, LTD. for "The Dance" from *Later Poems* by William Carlos Williams, for "Flowers by the Sea" from *Earlier Poems* by William Carlos Williams, and for "This is Just to Say" from *Earlier Poems* by William Carlos Williams. All reprinted by permission of the publishers.

THE MACMILLAN COMPANY for "Snow in the Suburbs" by Thomas Hardy from *Collected Poems* by Thomas Hardy, copyright, 1925, by The Macmillan Company, renewed 1953, by Lloyd's Bank, Ltd.; for "The Mysterious Cat" and "The Little Turtle" by Vachel Lindsay from *Collected Poems* by Vachel Lindsay, copyright, 1914, by The Macmillan Company, renewed 1942, by Elizabeth C. Lindsay, copyright, 1920, by The Macmillan Company, renewed 1948, by Elizabeth C. Lindsay; for "The Dark Hills" by Edwin Arlington Robinson from *Collected Poems* by Edwin Arlington Robinson, copyright, 1920, by The Macmillan Company, renewed 1948, by Ruth Nivison; for "Landscape as Metal and Flowers" by Winfield Townley Scott from *Collected Poems* by Winfield Townley Scott, copyright, 1937, 1941, by Winfield Townley Scott; for "The Goat Paths" by James Stephens from *Collected Poems* by James Stephens, copyright, 1915, by The Macmillan Company, renewed 1943, by James Stephens; for "Little Things" by James Stephens from *Collected Poems* by James Stephens, copyright, 1954, by The Macmillan Company; for "The Home" by Rabindranath Tagore from *The Crescent Moon: Child Poems* by Rabindranath Tagore, copyright, 1913, by The Macmillan Company, renewed 1941; for "The Song of Wandering Aengus," "Who Goes With Fergus," "When You Are Old" from *Collected Poems* by William Butler Yeats, copyright, 1906, by The Macmillan Company, renewed 1934, by William Butler Yeats; for "The Irish Airman Foresees His Death," "The Cat and the Moon" from *Collected Poems* by William Butler Yeats, copyright, 1919, by The Macmillan Company, renewed 1946, by Bertha Georgie Yeats; for "The Old Men Admiring Themselves in the Water" by William Butler Yeats from *Collected Poems* by William Butler Yeats, copyright, 1903, by The Macmillan Company, renewed 1931, by William Butler Yeats. All these poems included by permission of The Macmillan Company.

MACMILLAN & CO., LTD. (London) for the three poems by Thomas

Hardy from *The Collected Poems of Thomas Hardy*, reprinted by permission of the Trustees of the Hardy Estate and the publishers; for the two poems by James Stephens from *Collected Poems* by James Stephens, reprinted by permission of Mrs. Iris Wise and the publishers; for "The Home" from *The Crescent Moon* by Rabindranath Tagore, reprinted from *The Collected Poems and Plays of Rabindranath Tagore*, by permission of the Trustees of the Tagore Estate and the publishers.

MACMILLAN & CO., LTD. and ST. MARTIN'S PRESS, INC. for "The Bells of Heaven," "A Wood Song," and "A Song" from *Collected Poems* by Ralph Hodgson. Reprinted by permission of the publishers.

MRS. D. M. MEWTON-WOOD for "Romance" and "Song" by W. J. Turner.

SIR FRANCIS MEYNELL for "The Rainy Summer" by Alice Meynell.

C. R. MILNE and METHUEN & CO., LTD. for "The Three Foxes" by A. A. Milne from the book *When We Were Very Young* by A. A. Milne, copyright by C. R. Milne. Reprinted by permission of C. R. Milne and Methuen & Co., Ltd.

MRS. HAROLD MONRO for "Overheard on a Saltmarsh" by Harold Monro.

MISS MARIANNE MOORE for "A Talisman."

NEW DIRECTIONS for "There'd Be an Orchestra," stanza from the poem "Thousand-and-First Ship" by F. Scott Fitzgerald from *The Crack-Up* by F. Scott Fitzgerald, copyright, 1934, 1936, by Esquire, Inc., copyright, 1945, by New Directions; for "An Immorality" by Ezra Pound from *Personae* by Ezra Pound, copyright, 1926, 1954, by Ezra Pound; for "Fern Hill" by Dylan Thomas from *The Collected Poems of Dylan Thomas*, copyright, 1953, by Dylan Thomas, ©, 1957, by New Directions; and for "Johnnie Crack and Flossie Snail" from *Under Milk Wood* by Dylan Thomas, copyright, 1954, by New Directions; for the three poems by William Carlos Williams from *Selected Poems* by William Carlos Williams, copyright, 1938, by New Directions, copyright, 1944, 1948, 1949, by William Carlos Williams. All these poems reprinted by permission of New Directions.

THE NEW YORKER for "Just Dropped In" by William Cole, copyright, 1955, by *The New Yorker*, and for "Manhole Covers" by Karl Shapiro, copyright, 1962, by *The New Yorker*. Reprinted by permission of *The New Yorker*.

OXFORD UNIVERSITY PRESS, INC. for "Portrait of a Girl" from "Priapus and the Pool" by Conrad Aiken from *Collected Poems of Conrad Aiken*, copyright by Conrad Aiken; for "Pied Beauty" and "Spring and Fall" by Gerard Manley Hopkins, from *Poems of Gerard Manley Hopkins*, Third Edition, edited by W. H. Gardner, copyright, 1948, by Oxford University Press, Inc. All reprinted by permission of the publishers.

A. D. PETERS & CO. for "Sarah Byng" and "The Frog" by Hilaire Belloc. Reprinted by permission of A. D. Peters & Co.

LAURENCE POLLINGER, LTD. and JONATHAN CAPE, LTD. for the selections from *The Complete Poems of Robert Frost*, reprinted by permission of Laurence Pollinger, Ltd and. Jonathan Cape, Ltd.

LAURENCE POLLINGER, LTD. and THE ESTATE OF THE LATE MRS. FRIEDA LAWRENCE for "Bavarian Gentians" by D. H. Lawrence from *The Complete Poems of D. H. Lawrence*. Reprinted by permission of Laurence Pollinger, Ltd. and the Estate of the late Mrs. Frieda Lawrence (and the publishers, William Heinemann, Ltd.).

EZRA POUND for "An Immorality." Reprinted by permission of Ezra Pound and Mr. A. V. Moore, Mr. Pound's agent.

PUTNAM & COMPANY, LTD. for the poem by Isak Dinesen from *Out of Africa* by Isak Dinesen, copyright, 1937, by Putman & Company, Ltd. Reprinted by permission of the publishers.

RANDOM HOUSE, INC. for "Their Lonely Betters" by W. H. Auden from *Nones* by W. H. Auden, copyright, 1951, by W. H. Auden; for the poem by Isak Dinesen from *Out of Africa* by Isak Dinesen, copyright, 1937, 1938, by Random House, Inc.; for "The Express" by Stephen Spender from *Poems* by Stephen Spender, copyright, 1934, and renewed 1961, by Stephen Spender, reprinted from *Collected Poems 1928–1953* by Stephen Spender. All these poems reprinted by permission of Random House, Inc.

MRS. BEATRICE ROETHKE for "The Bat," copyright, 1938, 1939, by Theodore Roethke, "Big Wind," copyright, 1947, by United Chapters of Phi Beta Kappa, "The Lady and the Bear," copyright, 1951, by Theodore Roethke, all from *Words for the Wind*.

ST. MARTIN'S PRESS, INC. for "The Hammers" by Ralph Hodgson from *Collected Poems* by Ralph Hodgson. Reprinted by permission of St. Martin's Press, Inc.

CHARLES SCRIBNER'S SONS for "The Birds of Paradise" from *The Collected Poems* of John Peale Bishop, (p. 212), edited by Allen Tate, copyright, 1948, by Charles Scribner's Sons; and for "Ducks' Ditty" and "The Song of Mr. Toad" by Kenneth Grahame from *The Wind in the Willows* by Kenneth Grahame, copyright, 1908, 1933, by Charles Scribner's Sons; and for "The House on the Hill" by Edwin Arlington Robinson from *The Children of the Night* by Edwin Arlington Robinson, Charles Scribner's Sons, 1897. All these reprinted by permission of the publishers.

MARTIN SECKER & WARBURG, LTD. for "Stillness," "Santorin," and "The Golden Journey to Samarkand: Prologue" by James Elroy Flecker. Reprinted by permission of the publishers.

SIMON & SCHUSTER, INC. for "Deck Us All with Boston Charlie" by Walt Kelly, copyright, 1948, 1964, by Walt Kelly. Reprinted by permission of the publishers.

THE SOCIETY OF AUTHORS as the literary representative of the Estate of the late A. E. Housman and Jonathan Cape, Ltd., publishers of A. E. Housman's *Collected Poems*, for "Into My Heart" by A. E. Housman, reprinted by permission of The Society of Authors and Jonathan Cape, Ltd.; and for the selections by Walter de la Mare, all reprinted by permission of the Literary Trustees of Walter de la Mare and the Society of Authors as their representative.

MRS. HELEN THOMAS for the selections by Edward Thomas.

UNIVERSITY OF NEBRASKA PRESS for "Riddle #29: The Moon and the Sun," translated from the Old English by Burton Raffel from *Poems from the Old English*, translated by Burton Raffel, copyright, 1960, and 1964, by University of Nebraska Press. Reprinted by permission of the publishers.

THE VIKING PRESS, INC. for the selections by Elizabeth Madox Roberts from *Under The Tree* by Elizabeth Madox Roberts, copyright, 1922, by B. W. Huebsch, Inc., 1950, by Ivor S. Roberts; and for "Bavarian Gentians" by D. H. Lawrence from *The Complete Poems of D. H. Lawrence*, edited by Vivian de Sola Pinto and F. Warren Roberts, copyright, 1933 by Frieda Lawrence, © 1964 by Angelo Ravagli and F. Warren Roberts, Executors of the Estate of Mrs. Frieda Lawrence. All these poems reprinted by permission of The Viking Press, Inc.

FREDERICK WARNE & CO., LTD. for the poem by Beatrix Potter, copyright, 1917, by Frederick Warne & Co., Ltd.; and for "Little Wind" by Kate

Greenaway from *Under the Window* by Kate Greenaway. Reprinted by permission of Frederick Warne & Co., Ltd.

FRANKLIN WATTS, INC. for "Nursery Rhyme of Innocence and Experience" by Charles Causley, copyright, 1963, by Franklin Watts, Inc. Reprinted by permission of the publishers.

WESLEYAN UNIVERSITY PRESS for "The Base Stealer" by Robert Francis, copyright, 1948, by Robert Francis from *The Orb Weaver* by Robert Francis; for "Early Supper" by Barbara Howes, copyright, 1956, by Barbara Howes from *Light and Dark* by Barbara Howes; and for "At a Child's Baptism" by Vassar Miller, copyright, 1961, by Vassar Miller, from *My Bones Being Wiser* by Vassar Miller. All reprinted by permission of Wesleyan University Press. "Early Supper" by Barbara Howes appeared originally in *The New Yorker*.

EDMUND WILSON for "Peterhof" from *Night Thoughts* by Edmund Wilson.

MISS EUPHEMIA ANN WOLFE for the two poems by Humbert Wolfe.

MISS JUDITH WRIGHT and ANGUS AND ROBERTSON, LTD. (Sydney) for "Egrets" and "Lyrebirds" by Judith Wright from *Birds* by Judith Wright, copyright, 1963. Reprinted by permission of Judith Wright and the publishers.

MRS. W. B. YEATS and MACMILLAN & CO. LTD. (London) for the selection by William Butler Yeats from *Collected Poems of W. B. Yeats*. Reprinted by permission of Mrs. W. B. Yeats and Macmillan & Co., Ltd.

FOR

Maidie

and

David and Gregory

CONTENTS

Introduction	*xv*
The Home RABINDRANATH TAGORE	*xix*
WHAT IS PINK/*Rhymes*	*1*
SLIGHT THINGS	*17*
THE WIND AND THE RAIN	*31*
A PEA-GREEN GAMUT/*Country Poems*	*37*
BIRDS, BEASTS, AND FLOWERS	*61*
SPRING AND SUMMER	*93*
IN BETWEEN ARE THE PEOPLE	*103*
GO, LOVELY ROSE/*Love Poems*	*117*
MANY LOVE MUSIC	*129*
THEY WENT TO SEA IN A SIEVE/*Nonsense Verses*	*143*
BALLADS	*157*
THE SEA	*175*
THE DARK HILLS/*War Poems*	*187*
ALL THAT'S PAST	*195*
HERE AND NOW	*207*
LYREBIRD COUNTRY/*Dreams and Fancies*	*215*
WHEN YOU ARE OLD	*231*
THE MOON AND THE SUN	*239*
YEAR'S END	*247*
Author Index	*261*
Title Index	*269*

INTRODUCTION

The writing of poetry is one of the oldest and most complex of human activities, and because poetry—like life itself—is mysterious, any attempt to define it seems not only doomed to failure but also designed almost to destroy the nature of the thing. "As we go back in history," wrote Ralph Waldo Emerson "language becomes more picturesque, until in its infancy, when it is all poetry. . . ." The poet then is, like primitive man, an image-maker, a user of symbols. Since all language was spoken before it was written, the aural element in poetry is of prime importance: the word moved from the lip to the ear, and even today poetry may be said to begin with sound; the meaning follows. Primitive man instinctively gave form and pattern to the symbols he employed; poetry, therefore, at its very base, is a pattern of sound. Meter and rhyme help to make poetry easy to remember; and, because of its sound pattern or design, poetry is able to express many kinds of emotion which prose cannot convey. The metrical beat of a line of verse reminds us, as well, of the dance; and music and dancing have been associated with poetry since primitive times.

The novelist Isak Dinesen tells of reciting English poetry to the natives of Kenya; although they understood nothing, they were enchanted by what they heard and begged her to recite more, or, in their words, to speak like rain. The pleasure to be found in the ingenious use of rhyme and meter goes far back in time. Thousands of years before the invention of printing men, women, and children delighted in spoken verse. The compositions of the poets or bards were the chief sources of entertainment among all kinds of people. Some poetry could not be assigned to this poet or that; and much of this anonymous verse has come down to us in the form of songs or of story-telling ballads. This spoken verse was often thought to possess magical qualities; we come upon rhymed runes and spells, the age-old meaning of which has been forgotten. Mother Goose rhymes are also, in many cases, very ancient indeed; and the origin of children's counting-out rhymes, and other rhymes attached to games, is often so old as to be unknown today.

Robert Frost said of a poem that it "begins in delight and ends in wisdom," and further that it "assumes direction with the first line laid down, it runs a course of lucky events, and ends in a clarification of life—not necessarily a great clarification, such as sects and cults are founded on, but in a momentary stay against confusion." The delight—the pleasure in sound, imagery, measured rhythm—comes first. Our understanding of the poem's logical meaning comes next. Sometimes there is no logical meaning whatever; the poem is a piece of nonsense, a riddle, or a joke. We must not be solemn about poetry; it reflects life, and life is many-colored. But poetry can, even in its lightest aspects, clarify life. One of Robert Frost's earliest and most delicate poems is concerned with cleaning a pasture spring; the title of his last volume is *In the Clearing*. His life-long preoccupation with clarification will, we hope, offer an inspiration to those of our young readers who encounter in this anthology for the first time a number of his poems.

The theme of pilgrimage and of quest appears again and again in myth and fairy-tale. The reading of poetry of different times and places resembles in itself an imaginary journey; and we have taken our title from a poem by a twentieth-century British poet who had traveled in the Middle East, "The Golden Journey to Samarkand," by James Elroy Flecker. The poet is a traveler whose itinerary covers every area of human experience from birth to death. His only preparation for his journey is reality, his only map is that traced out for him by his imagination, his only equipment—the entire assembly of his luggage—consists in the tools of his craft. But still he can take us, as Keats said, "in realms of gold." The poet goes back and forth over the same territory as other men in their day to day occupations, in their struggle for survival, in their delight and dismay at life. But he sees more and he tells more; he takes us to far-off places we have seen only in dreams or to nearby places we have visited but, in the deepest sense, never reached.

The poems we have selected cover a wide range—all the way from simple rhymes on the slightest of subjects to supreme flights of the imagination. Some were written by the greatest poets of the past, British and American; others are the work of recent, and, in some cases, unknown poets. Many have never before been collected; others are here printed for the first time. We have included, with one or two exceptions, nothing of unknown authorship, only because so many anonymous rhymes and ballads are available in other collections; and we have in general refrained from using translations and from excerpting from long poems.

Fashions in poetry, like fashions in dress, are subject to constant change, but we have in our selection tried to cut through fashion and to present our readers with poems that have survived past evolutions of taste and others that seem destined to live beyond the taste of today. We have offered only poems that we have ourselves enjoyed and read and remembered with pleasure: old and new poems; poems written in English, but written, sometimes in far countries, such as Australia; poems about many and diverse subjects—but always, we feel, poems fresh, delightful, and perennially new.

LOUISE BOGAN
WILLIAM JAY SMITH

THE HOME

I paced alone on the road across the field
while the sunset was hiding its last gold
like a miser.

The daylight sank deeper and deeper into the
darkness, and the widowed land, whose harvest
had been reaped, lay silent.

Suddenly a boy's shrill voice rose into the sky.
He traversed the dark unseen, leaving the track
of his song across the hush of the evening.

His village home lay there at the end of
the waste land, beyond the sugar-cane field,
hidden among the shadows of the banana
and the slender areca palm, the cocoa-nut and
the dark green jack-fruit trees.

I stopped for a moment in my lonely way
under the starlight, and saw spread before
me the darkened earth surrounding with her
arms countless homes furnished with cradles
and beds, mothers' hearts and evening lamps,
and young lives glad with a gladness that
knows nothing of its value for the world.

RABINDRANATH TAGORE

WHAT IS PINK?

Rhymes

WHAT IS PINK?

What is pink? a rose is pink
By the fountain's brink.
What is red? a poppy's red
In its barley bed.
What is blue? the sky is blue
Where the clouds float thro'
What is white? a swan is white
Sailing in the light.
What is yellow? pears are yellow,
Rich and ripe and mellow.
What is green? the grass is green,
With small flowers between.
What is violet? clouds are violet
In the summer twilight.
What is orange? why, an orange,
Just an orange!

CHRISTINA ROSSETTI

PICNIC

Ella, fell a
Maple tree.
Hilda, build a
Fire for me.

Teresa, squeeze a
Lemon, so.
Amanda, hand a
Plate to Flo.

Nora, pour a
Cup of tea.
Fancy, Nancy
What a spree!

HUGH LOFTING

GRIZZLY BEAR

If you ever, ever, ever meet a grizzly bear,
You must never, never, never ask him *where*
He is going.
Or *what* he is doing;
For if you ever, ever, dare
To stop a grizzly bear,
You will never meet *another* grizzly bear.

MARY AUSTIN

TEAPOTS AND QUAILS

Teapots and Quails,
Snuffers and snails,
Set him a sailing
and see how he sails!

*

Mitres and beams,
Thimbles and Creams,
Set him a screaming
and hark! how he screams!

*

Ribands and Pigs,
Helmets and Figs,
Set him a jigging
and see how he jigs!

*

Tadpoles and Tops,
Teacups and Mops,
Set him a hopping
and see how he hops!

*

Lobsters and owls,
Scissors and fowls,
Set him a howling
and hark how he howls!

*

Eagles and pears,
Slippers and Bears,
Set him a staring
and see how he stares!

*

Sofas and bees,
Camels and Keys,
Set him a sneezing
and see how he'll sneeze!

*

Thistles and Moles,
Crumpets and Soles,
Set it a rolling
and see how it rolls!

*

Hurdles and Mumps,
Poodles and pumps,
Set it a jumping
and see how he jumps!

*

Pancakes and Fins,
Roses and Pins,
Set him a grinning
and see how he grins!

EDWARD LEAR

COUNTING-OUT RHYME

Silver bark of beech, and sallow
Bark of yellow birch and yellow
   Twig of willow.

Stripe of green in moosewood maple,
Colour seen in leaf of apple,
   Bark of popple.

Wood of popple pale as moonbeam,
Wood of oak for yoke and barn-beam,
   Wood of hornbeam.

Silver bark of beech, and hollow
Stem of elder, tall and yellow
   Twig of willow.

      EDNA ST. VINCENT MILLAY

ELETELEPHONY

Once there was an elephant,
Who tried to use the telephant—
No! no! I mean an elephone
Who tried to use the telephone—
(Dear me! I am not certain quite
That even now I've got it right.)

Howe'er it was, he got his trunk
Entangled in the telephunk;
The more he tried to get it free,
The louder buzzed the telephee—
(I fear I'd better drop the song
Of elephop and telephong!)

LAURA RICHARDS

THE OLD WOMAN

You know the old woman
    Who lived in a shoe?
And had so many children
    She didn't know what to do?

I think if she lived in
    A little shoe-house—
That little old woman was
    Surely a mouse!

BEATRIX POTTER

LIMERICKS

There was an Old Man with a gong,
Who bumped at it all the day long;
But they called out, "O law! you're a horrid old bore!"
So they smashed that Old Man with a gong.

*

There was a Young Lady whose eyes,
Were unique as to color and size;
When she opened them wide, people all turned aside,
And started away in surprise.

*

There was an Old Man who said, "Hush!
I perceive a young bird in this bush!"
When they said—"Is it small?" He replied—"Not at all!
It is four times as big as the bush!"

*

There was an old person of Diss,
Who said, "It is this! It is this!"
When they said "What? or which?"—He jumped into a ditch,
Which absorbed that old person of Diss.

EDWARD LEAR

THE FROG

Be kind and tender to the Frog
    And do not call him names,
As "Slimy skin," or "Polly-wog,"
    Or likewise "Ugly James,"
Or "Gap-a-grin," or "Toad-gone-wrong,"
    Or "Bill Bandy-knees":
The Frog is justly sensitive
    To epithets like these.
No animal will more repay
    A treatment kind and fair
At least so lonely people say
Who keep a frog (and, by the way,
They are extremely rare).

HILAIRE BELLOC

HENRY AND MARY

Henry was a young king,
    Mary was his queen;
He gave her a snowdrop
    On a stalk of green.

>   Then all for his kindness
>   And all for his care
>   She gave him a new-laid egg
>   In the garden there.
>
>   "Love, can you sing?"
>   "I cannot sing."
>   "Or tell a tale?"
>   "Not one I know."
>   "Then let us play at queen and king
>   As down the garden walks we go."

ROBERT GRAVES

FERRY ME ACROSS THE WATER

> "Ferry me across the water,
>   Do, boatman, do."
> "If you've a penny in your purse
>   I'll ferry you."

"I have a penny in my purse,
    And my eyes are blue;
So ferry me across the water,
    Do, boatman, do!"

"Step into my ferry-boat,
    Be they black or blue,
And for the penny in your purse
    I'll ferry you."

CHRISTINA ROSSETTI

THE THREE FOXES

Once upon a time there were three little foxes
Who didn't wear stockings, and they didn't wear sockses,
But they all had handkerchiefs to blow their noses,
And they kept their handkerchiefs in cardboard boxes.

They lived in the forest in three little houses,
And they didn't wear coats, and they didn't wear trousies.
They ran through the woods on their little bare tootsies,
And they played "Touch last" with a family of mouses.

They didn't go shopping in the High Street shopses,
But caught what they wanted in the woods and copses.
They all went fishing, and they caught three wormses,
They went out hunting, and they caught three wopses.

They went to a Fair, and they all won prizes—
Three plum-puddingses and three mince-pieses.
They rode on elephants and swang on swingses,
And hit three coco-nuts at coco-nut shieses.

That's all that I know of the three little foxes
Who kept their handkerchiefs in cardboard boxes.
They lived in the forest in three little houses,
But they didn't wear coats and they didn't wear trousies,
And they didn't wear stockings and they didn't wear sockses.

A. A. MILNE

THE LAST WORD OF A BLUEBIRD

(As Told to a Child)

As I went out a Crow
In a low voice said "Oh,
I was looking for you.
How do you do?
I just came to tell you
To tell Lesley (will you?)
That her little Bluebird
Wanted me to bring word
That the north wind last night
That made the stars bright
And made ice on the trough

Almost made him cough
His tail feathers off.
He just had to fly!
But he sent her Good-bye,
And said to be good,
And wear her red hood,
And look for skunk tracks
In the snow with an axe—
And do everything!
And perhaps in the spring
He would come back and sing."

ROBERT FROST

THE OWL AND THE PUSSY CAT

The Owl and the Pussy cat went to sea
   In a beautiful pea-green boat:
They took some honey, and plenty of money
   Wrapped up in a five-pound note.
The Owl looked up to the stars above,
   And sang to a small guitar,
   "O lovely Pussy, O Pussy, my love,
   What a beautiful Pussy you are,
         You are,
         You are!
   What a beautiful Pussy you are!"

Pussy said to the Owl, "You elegant fowl,
    How charmingly sweet you sing!
Oh! let us be married; too long we have tarried:
    But what shall we do for a ring?"
They sailed away, for a year and a day
    To the land where the bong-tree grows,
And there in a wood a Piggy-wig stood,
    With a ring at the end of his nose,
          His nose,
          His nose,
    With a ring at the end of his nose.

"Dear Pig, are you willing to sell for one shilling
    Your ring?" Said the Piggy, "I will."
So they took it away, and were married next day
    By the Turkey who lives on the hill.
They dinèd on mince and slices of quince,
    Which they ate with a runcible spoon,
And hand in hand, on the edge of the sand,
    They danced by the light of the moon,
          The moon,
          The moon,
    They danced by the light of the moon.

EDWARD LEAR

SLIGHT THINGS

LITTLE THINGS

Little things that run and quail
And die in silence and despair;

Little things that fight and fail
And fall on earth and sea and air;

All trapped and frightened little things
The mouse, the coney, hear our prayer.

As we forgive those done to us,
The lamb, the linnet, and the hare,

Forgive us all our trespasses,
Little creatures everywhere.

JAMES STEPHENS

THE BELLS OF HEAVEN

'Twould ring the bells of Heaven
The wildest peal for years,
If Parson lost his senses
And people came to theirs,
And he and they together
Knelt down with angry prayers
For tamed and shabby tigers
And dancing dogs and bears,
And wretched, blind pit ponies,
And little hunted hares.

RALPH HODGSON

IF I SHOULD EVER BY CHANCE

If I should ever by chance grow rich
I'll buy Codham, Cockridden, and Childerditch,
Roses, Pyrgo, and Lapwater,
And let them all to my elder daughter.
The rent I shall ask of her will be only
Each year's first violets, white and lonely,
The first primroses and orchises—
She must find them before I do, that is.
But if she finds a blossom on furze
Without rent they shall all for ever be hers,
Whenever I am sufficiently rich:

Codham, Cockridden, and Childerditch,
Roses, Pyrgo and Lapwater—
I shall give them all to my elder daughter.

EDWARD THOMAS

HIS GRANGE, OR PRIVATE WEALTH

Though Clock,
To tell how night drawes hence, I've none,
A Cock,
I have, to sing how day drawes on.
I have
A maid (my *Prew*) by good luck sent,
To save
That little, Fates me gave or lent.
A Hen
I keep, which creeking day by day,
Tells when
She goes her long white egg to lay.
A Goose
I have, which, with a jealous eare,
Lets loose
Her tongue, to tell what danger's neare.
A Lamb
I keep (tame) with my morsells fed,
Whose Dam
An Orphan left him (lately dead.)

A Cat
I keep, that playes about my House,
Grown fat,
With eating many a miching Mouse.
To these
A *Trasy** I do keep, whereby
I please
The more my rurall privacie:
Which are
But toyes, to give my heart some ease:
Where care
None is, slight things do lightly please.

ROBERT HERRICK

MISS T.

It's a very odd thing—
　　As odd as can be—
That whatever Miss T. eats
　　Turns into Miss T.;
Porridge and apples,
　　Mince, muffins, and mutton,
Jam, junket, jumbles—
　　Not a rap, not a button
It matters; the moment
　　They're out of her plate,
Though shared by Miss Butcher

* *His Spaniel*

And sour Mr. Bate,
Tiny and cheerful,
And neat as can be,
Whatever Miss T. eats
Turns into Miss T.

WALTER DE LA MARE

BUNCHES OF GRAPES

"Bunches of grapes," says Timothy;
　"Pomegranates pink," says Elaine;
"A junket of cream and a cranberry tart
　For me," says Jane.

"Love-in-a-mist," says Timothy;
　"Primroses pale," says Elaine;
"A nosegay of pinks and mignonette
　For me," says Jane.

"Chariots of gold," says Timothy;
　"Silvery wings," says Elaine;
"A bumpity ride in a wagon of hay
　For me," says Jane.

WALTER DE LA MARE

A TERNARIE OF LITTLES, UPON A PIPKIN OF JELLIE SENT TO A LADY

1   A little Saint best fits a little Shrine,
    A little prop best fits a little Vine,
    As my small Cruse best fits my little Wine.

2   A little Seed best fits a little Soyle,
    A little Trade best fits a little Toyle:
    As my small Jarre best fits my little Oyle.

3   A little Bin best fits a little Bread,
    A little Garland fits a little Head:
    As my small stuffe best fits my little Shed.

4   A little Hearth best fits a little Fire,
    A little Chappell fits a little Quire,
    As my small Bell best fits my little Spire.

5   A little streame best fits a little Boat;
    A little lead best fits a little Float;
    As my small Pipe best fits my little note.

6   A little meat best fits a little bellie,
    As sweetly Lady, give me leave to tell ye,
    This little Pipkin fits this little Jellie.

ROBERT HERRICK

THE SWING

How do you like to go up in a swing,
    Up in the air so blue?
Oh, I do think it the pleasantest thing
    Ever a child can do!

Up in the air and over the wall,
    Till I can see so wide,
Rivers and trees and cattle and all
    Over the countryside—

Till I look down on the garden green,
    Down on the roof so brown—
Up in the air I go flying again,
    Up in the air and down!

ROBERT LOUIS STEVENSON

THE BARBER'S

Gold locks, and black locks,
    Red locks and brown,
Topknot to love-curl,
    The hair wisps down;
Straight above the clear eyes,
    Rounded round the ears,
Snip-snap and snick-a-snick,
    Clash the Barber's shears;

Us, in the looking-glass,
    Footsteps in the street,
Over, under, to and fro,
    The lean blades meet;
Bay Rum or Bear's Grease,
    A silver groat to pay—
Then out a-shin-shan-shining
    In the bright, blue day.

WALTER DE LA MARE

THE MOUNTAIN AND THE SQUIRREL

The mountain and the squirrel
Had a quarrel,
And the former called the latter "Little prig":
Bun replied,
"You are doubtless very big;
But all sorts of things and weather
Must be taken in together
To make up a year,
And a sphere.
And I think it no disgrace
To occupy my place.
If I'm not so large as you,
You are not so small as I,
And not half so spry:
I'll not deny you make

A very pretty squirrel track.
Talents differ; all is well and wisely put;
If I cannot carry forests on my back,
Neither can you crack a nut."

RALPH WALDO EMERSON

EARLY SUPPER

Laughter of children brings
    The kitchen down with laughter.
While the old kettle sings
Laughter of children brings
To a boil all savory things.
    Higher than beam or rafter,
Laughter of children brings
    The kitchen down with laughter.

So ends an autumn day,
    Light ripples on the ceiling,
Dishes are stacked away;
So ends an autumn day,
The children jog and sway
    In comic dances wheeling.
So ends an autumn day,
    Light ripples on the ceiling.

They trail upstairs to bed,
    And night is a dark tower.
The kettle calls: instead
They trail upstairs to bed,
Leaving warmth, the coppery-red
    Mood of their carnival hour.
They trail upstairs to bed,
    And night is a dark tower.

BARBARA HOWES

AT A CHILD'S BAPTISM

For Sarah Elizabeth

Hold her softly, not for long
Love lies sleeping on your arm,
Shyer than a bird in song,
Quick to fly off in alarm.

It is well that you are wise,
Knowing she for whom you care
Is not yours as prey or prize,
No more to be owned than air.

To your wisdom you add grace,
Which will give your child release
From the ark of your embrace
That she may return with peace

Till she joins the elemental.
God Himself now holds your daughter
Softly, too, by this most gentle
Rein of all, this drop of water.

VASSAR MILLER

ANOTHER GRACE FOR A CHILD

Here a little child I stand,
Heaving up my either hand;
Cold as Paddocks* though they be,
Here I lift them up to Thee,
For a Benizon to fall
On our meat, and on us all. *Amen.*

ROBERT HERRICK

* Paddocks: *frogs*

THE WIND AND THE RAIN

WHO HAS SEEN THE WIND?

Who has seen the wind?
   Neither I nor you;
But when the leaves hang trembling
   The wind is passing thro'.

Who has seen the wind?
   Neither you nor I;
But when the trees bow down their heads
   The wind is passing by.

CHRISTINA ROSSETTI

LITTLE WIND

Little wind, blow on the hill-top;
Little wind, blow down the plain;
Little wind, blow up the sunshine,
Little wind, blow off the rain.

KATE GREENAWAY

RAIN

The rain is raining all around,
    It falls on field and tree,
It rains on the umbrellas here,
    And on the ships at sea.

ROBERT LOUIS STEVENSON

I SAW THE WIND TODAY

I saw the wind to-day:
I saw it in the pane
Of glass upon the wall:
A moving thing,—'twas like
No bird with widening wing,
No mouse that runs along
The meal bag under the beam.

I think it like a horse,
All black, with frightening mane,
That springs out of the earth,
And tramples on his way.
I saw it in the glass,
The shaking of a mane:
A horse that no one rides!

PADRAIC COLUM

THE WIND AND THE MOON

Said the Wind to the Moon,
"I will blow you out;
    You stare
    In the air
    Like a ghost in a chair
Always looking what I am about.
I hate to be watched—I'll blow you out."

GEORGE MACDONALD

WINDY NIGHTS

Whenever the moon and stars are set,
    Whenever the wind is high,
All night long in the dark and wet,
    A man goes riding by.
Late in the night when the fires are out,
    Why does he gallop and gallop about?

Whenever the trees are crying aloud,
    And ships are tossed at sea,
By, on the highway, low and loud,
    By at the gallop goes he.
By at the gallop he goes, and then
    By he comes back at the gallop again.

ROBERT LOUIS STEVENSON

A PEA-GREEN GAMUT

Country Poems

COLD ARE THE CRABS

Cold are the crabs that crawl on yonder hills,
Colder the cucumbers that grow beneath,
And colder still the brazen chops that wreathe
   The tedious gloom of philosophic pills!
For when the tardy film of nectar fills
The ample bowls of demons and of men,
There lurks the feeble mouse, the homely hen,
   And there the porcupine with all her quills.
Yet much remains—to weave a solemn strain
That lingering sadly—slowly dies away,
Daily departing with departing day.
A pea green gamut on a distant plain
When wily walrusses in congress meet—
   Such such is life—

                EDWARD LEAR

MINNIE AND MATTIE

Minnie and Mattie
    And fat little May,
Out in the country,
    Spending a day.

Such a bright day,
    With the sun glowing,
And the trees half in leaf,
    And the grass growing.

Pinky white pigling
    Squeals through his snout,
Woolly white lambkin
    Frisks all about,

Cluck! cluck! the nursing hen
    Summons her folk,—
Ducklings all downy soft,
    Yellow as yolk.

Cluck! cluck! the mother hen
    Summons her chickens
To peck the dainty bits
    Found in her pickings.

Minnie and Mattie
    And May carry posies,
Half of sweet violets,
    Half of primroses.

CHRISTINA ROSSETTI

LAUGHING SONG

When the green woods laugh with the voice of joy,
And the dimpling stream runs laughing by;
When the air does laugh with our merry wit,
And the green hill laughs with the noise of it;

When the meadows laugh with lively green,
And the grasshopper laughs in the merry scene,
When Mary and Susan and Emily
With their sweet round mouth sing "Ha, Ha, He!"

When the painted birds laugh in the shade,
When our table with cherries and nuts is spread,
Come live and be merry, and join with me,
To sing the sweet chorus of "Ha, Ha, He!"

WILLIAM BLAKE

THE HORSES OF THE SEA

The horses of the sea
    Rear a foaming crest,
But the horses of the land
    Serve us best.

The horses of the land
    Munch corn and clover,
While the foaming sea-horses
    Toss and turn over.

CHRISTINA ROSSETTI

THE BROOK

I come from haunts of coot and tern,
    I make a sudden sally,
And sparkle out among the fern,
    To bicker down a valley.

By thirty hills I hurry down,
    Or slip between the ridges,
By twenty thorps, a little town,
    And half a hundred bridges.

Till last by Philip's farm I flow
    To join the brimming river,
For men may come and men may go,
    But I go on for ever.

I chatter over stony ways,
  In little sharps and trebles,
I bubble into eddying bays,
  I babble on the pebbles.

With many a curve my banks I fret
  By many a field and fallow,
And many a fairy foreland set
  With willow-weed and mallow.

I chatter, chatter, as I flow,
  To join the brimming river,
For men may come and men may go,
  But I go on for ever.

I wind about, and in and out,
  With here a blossom sailing,
And here and there a lusty trout
  And here and there a grayling,

And here and there a foamy flake
  Upon me, as I travel
With many a silver water-break
  Above the golden gravel,

And draw them all along, and flow
  To join the brimming river,
For men may come and men may go,
  But I go on for ever.

I steal by lawns and grassy plots,
    I slide by hazel covers;
I move the sweet forget-me-nots
    That grow for happy lovers.

I slip, I slide, I gloom, I glance,
    Among my skimming swallows;
I make the netted sunbeam dance
    Against my sandy shallows.

I murmur under moon and stars
    In brambly wildernesses;
I linger by my shingly bars;
    I loiter round my cresses;

And out again I curve and flow
    To join the brimming river,
For men may come and men may go,
    But I go on for ever.

ALFRED, LORD TENNYSON

THE PASTURE

I'm going out to clean the pasture spring;
I'll only stop to rake the leaves away
(And wait to watch the water clear, I may):
I shan't be gone long.—You come too.

I'm going out to fetch the little calf
That's standing by the mother. It's so young,
It totters when she licks it with her tongue.
I shan't be gone long.—You come too.

ROBERT FROST

MILKING TIME

When supper time is almost come,
But not quite here, I cannot wait,
And so I take my china mug
And go down by the milking gate.

The cow is always eating shucks
And spilling off the little silk.
Her purple eyes are big and soft—
She always smells like milk.

And Father takes my mug from me,
And then he makes the stream come out.
I see it going in my mug
And foaming all about.

And when it's piling very high,
And when some little streams commence
To run and drip along the sides,
He hands it to me through the fence.

ELIZABETH MADOX ROBERTS

THE CORNFIELD

I went across the pasture lot
When not a one was watching me.
Away beyond the cattle barns
I climbed a little crooked tree.

And I could look down on the field
And see the corn and how it grows
Across the world and up and down
In very straight and even rows.

And far away and far away—
I wonder if the farmer man
Knows all about the corn and how
It comes together like a fan.

ELIZABETH MADOX ROBERTS

PIED BEAUTY

Glory be to God for dappled things—
    For skies of couple-color as a brinded cow;
        For rose-moles all in stipple upon trout that swim;
Fresh-firecoal chestnut-falls; finches' wings;
    Landscapes plotted and pieced—fold, fallow, and plow;
        And all trades, their gear and tackle and trim.
All things counter, original, spare, strange;
    Whatever is fickle, freckled (who knows how?)
        With swift, slow; sweet, sour; adazzle, dim;
He fathers-forth whose beauty is past change:
    Praise Him.

GERARD MANLEY HOPKINS

FIRST SONG

Then it was dusk in Illinois, the small boy
After an afternoon of carting dung
Hung on the rail fence, a sapped thing
Weary to crying. Dark was growing tall
And he began to hear the pond frogs all
Calling upon his ear with what seemed their joy.

Soon their sound was pleasant for a boy
Listening in the smoky dusk and the nightfall
Of Illinois, and then from the field two small
Boys came bearing cornstalk violins

And rubbed three cornstalk bows with resins,
And they set fiddling with them as with joy.

It was now fine music the frogs and the boys
Did in the towering Illinois twilight make
And into dark in spite of a right arm's ache
A boy's hunched body loved out of a stalk
The first song of his happiness, and the song woke
His heart to the darkness and into the sadness of joy.

GALWAY KINNELL

THE BUTTERBEAN TENT

All through the garden I went and went,
And I walked in under the butterbean tent.

The poles leaned up like a good tepee
And made a nice little house for me.

I had a hard brown clod for a seat,
And all outside was a cool green street.

A little green worm and a butterfly
And a cricket-like thing that could hop went by.

Hidden away there were flocks and flocks
Of bugs that could go like little clocks.

Such a good day it was when I spent
A long, long while in the butterbean tent.

ELIZABETH MADOX ROBERTS

THE OLD TREE

The wood shakes in the breeze
    Lifting its antlered heads;
Green leaf nor brown one sees
    But the rain's glassy beads.

One tree-trunk in the wood
    No tangled head uprears,
A stump of soft touchwood
    Dead to all hopes and fears.

Even the round-faced owl
    That shakes out his long hooting
With the moon cheek-a-jowl
    Could claw there no safe footing.

Riddled by worms' small shot,
    Empty of all desire,
It smoulders in its rot,
    A pillar of damp fire.

ANDREW YOUNG

DUCK'S DITTY

All along the backwater,
Through the rushes tall,
Ducks are a-dabbling,
Up tails all!

Ducks' tails, drakes' tails,
Yellow feet a-quiver,
Yellow bills all out of sight
Busy in the river!

Slushy green undergrowth
Where the roach swim—
Here we keep our larder,
Cool and full and dim!

Every one for what he likes!
We like to be
Heads down, tails up,
Dabbling free!

High in the blue above
Swifts whirl and call—
We are down a-dabbling
Up tails all!

KENNETH GRAHAME

THE HENS

The night was coming very fast;
It reached the gate as I ran past.

The pigeons had gone to the tower of the church
And all the hens were on their perch,

Up in the barn, and I thought I heard
A piece of a little purring word.

I stopped inside, waiting and staying,
To try to hear what the hens were saying.

They were asking something, that was plain,
Asking it over and over again.

One of them moved and turned around,
Her feathers made a ruffled sound,

A ruffled sound, like a bushful of birds,
And she said her little asking words.

She pushed her head close into her wing,
But nothing answered anything.

ELIZABETH MADOX ROBERTS

PLOUGHING ON SUNDAY

The white cock's tail
Tosses in the wind.
The turkey-cock's tail
Glitters in the sun.

Water in the fields.
The wind pours down.
The feathers flare
And bluster in the wind.

Remus, blow your horn!
I'm ploughing on Sunday,
Ploughing North America.
Blow your horn!

Tum-ti-tum,
Ti-tum-tum-tum!
The turkey-cock's tail
Spreads to the sun.

The white cock's tail
Streams to the moon.
Water in the fields.
The wind pours down.

WALLACE STEVENS

CAPE ANN

O quick quick quick, quick hear the song-sparrow,
Swamp-sparrow, fox-sparrow, vesper-sparrow
At dawn and dusk. Follow the dance
Of the goldfinch at noon. Leave to chance
The Blackburnian warbler, the shy one. Hail
With shrill whistle the note of the quail, the bob-white
Dodging by bay-bush. Follow the feet
Of the walker, the water-thrush. Follow the flight
Of the dancing arrow, the purple martin. Greet
In silence the bulbat. All are delectable. Sweet sweet sweet
But resign this land at the end, resign it
To its true owner, the tough one, the sea-gull.
The palaver is finished.

T. S. ELIOT

FERN HILL

Now as I was young and easy under the apple boughs
About the lilting house and happy as the grass was green,
　The night above the dingle starry,
　　Time let me hail and climb
　Golden in the heydays of his eyes,
And honoured among wagons I was prince of the apple towns

And once below a time I lordly had the trees and leaves
    Trail with daisies and barley
Down the rivers of the windfall light.

And as I was green and carefree, famous among the barns
About the happy yard and singing as the farm was home,
    In the sun that is young once only,
        Time let me play and be
    Golden in the mercy of his means,
And green and golden I was huntsman and herdsman, the calves
Sang to my horn, the foxes on the hills barked clear and cold,
    And the sabbath rang slowly
In the pebbles of the holy streams.

All the sun long it was running, it was lovely, the hay
Fields high as the house, the tunes from the chimneys, it was air
    And playing, lovely and watery
        And fire green as grass.
    And nightly under the simple stars
As I rode to sleep the owls were bearing the farm away,
All the moon long, I heard, blessed among stables, the nightjars
    Flying with the ricks, and the horses
        Flashing into the dark.

And then to awake, and the farm, like a wanderer white
With the dew, come back, the cock on his shoulder: it was all
    Shining, it was Adam and maiden,
        The sky gathered again
    And the sun grew round that very day.

So it must have been after the birth of the simple light
In the first, spinning place, the spellbound horses walking warm
   Out of the whinnying green stable
      On to the fields of praise.

And honoured among foxes and pheasants by the gay house
Under the new made clouds and happy as the heart was long,
   In the sun born over and over,
      I ran my heedless ways,
   My wishes raced through the house high hay
And nothing I cared, at my sky blue trades, that time allows
In all his tuneful turning so few and such morning songs
   Before the children green and golden
      Follow him out of grace.

Nothing I cared, in the lamb white days, that time would take me
Up to the swallow thronged loft by the shadow of my head,
   In the moon that is always rising,
      Nor that riding to sleep
   I should hear him fly with the high fields
And wake to the farm forever fled from the childless land.
Oh as I was young and easy in the mercy of his means,
      Time held me green and dying
   Though I sang in my chains like the sea.

DYLAN THOMAS

THE GOAT PATHS

I

The crooked paths
Go every way
Upon the hill
—They wind about
Through the heather,
In and out
Of a quiet
Sunniness.
And the goats,
Day after day,
Stray
In sunny
Quietness;
Cropping here,
And cropping there
—As they pause,
And turn,
And pass—
Now a bit
Of heather spray,
Now a mouthful
Of the grass.

II

In the deeper
Sunniness;
In the place
Where nothing stirs;
Quietly
In quietness;
In the quiet
Of the furze
They stand a while;
They dream;
They lie;
They stare
Upon the roving sky.

If you approach
They run away!
They will stare,
And stamp,
And bound,
With a sudden angry sound,
To the sunny
Quietude;
To crouch again,
Where nothing stirs,
In the quiet
Of the furze:

To crouch them down again,
And brood,
In the sunny
Solitude.

III

Were I but
As free
As they,
I would stray
Away
And brood;
I would beat
A hidden way,
Through the quiet
Heather spray,
To a sunny
Solitude.

And should you come
I'd run away!
I would make an angry sound,
I would stare,
And stamp,
And bound
To the deeper
Quietude;

To the place
Where nothing stirs
In the quiet
Of the furze.

IV

In that airy
Quietness
I would dream
As long as they:
Through the quiet
Sunniness
I would stray
Away
And brood,
All among
The heather spray,
In a sunny
Solitude.

—I would think
Until I found
Something I can never find;
—Something
Lying
On the ground,
In the bottom
Of my mind.

JAMES STEPHENS

BIRDS, BEASTS AND

FLOWERS

EGRETS

Once as I travelled through a quiet evening,
I saw a pool, jet-black and mirror still.
Beyond, the slender paperbarks stood crowding;
each on its own white image looked its fill,
and nothing moved but thirty egrets wading—
thirty egrets in a quiet evening.

Once in a lifetime, lovely past believing,
your lucky eyes may light on such a pool.
As though for many years I had been waiting,
I watched in silence, till my heart was full
of clear dark water, and white trees unmoving,
and, whiter yet, those egrets wading.

JUDITH WRIGHT

THE LAMB

    Little lamb, who made thee?
    Dost thou know who made thee?
Gave thee life, and bid thee feed
By the stream and o'er the mead;
Gave thee clothing of delight,
Softest clothing, woolly, bright;
Gave thee such a tender voice,
Making all the vales rejoice?
    Little lamb, who made thee?
    Dost thou know who made thee?

    Little lamb, I'll tell thee;
    Little lamb, I'll tell thee;
He is calléd by thy name,
For He calls Himself a Lamb,
He is meek, and he is mild,
He became a little child,
I a child, and thou a lamb
We are called by his name.
    Little lamb, God bless thee!
    Little lamb, God bless thee!

                WILLIAM BLAKE

THE GRAY SQUIRREL

Like a small gray
coffee-pot
sits the squirrel.
He is not
all he should be,
kills by dozens
trees, and eats
his red-brown cousins.

The keeper, on the
other hand
, who shot him, is
a Christian, and

loves his enemies,
which shows
the squirrel was not
one of those.

HUMBERT WOLFE

A NARROW FELLOW IN THE GRASS

A narrow fellow in the grass
Occasionally rides;
You may have met him,—did you not?
His notice sudden is.

The grass divides as with a comb,
A spotted shaft is seen;
And then it closes at your feet
And opens further on.

He likes a boggy acre,
A floor too cool for corn.
Yet when a child, and barefoot,
I more than once, at morn,

Have passed, I thought, a whip-lash
Unbraiding in the sun,—
When, stooping to secure it,
It wrinkled, and was gone.

Several of nature's people
I know, and they know me;
I feel for them a transport
Of cordiality;

But never met this fellow,
Attended or alone,
Without a tighter breathing,
And zero at the bone.

EMILY DICKINSON

THE BIRDS OF PARADISE

I have seen the Birds of Paradise
   Afloat in the heavy noon,
Their irised plumes, their trailing gold,
Their crested heads, like flames grown cold;
   They rose and vanished soon.

Strange dust is blown into mine eyes;
   I doubt I shall ever see
Their lightly lifted forms again,
Their burning plumes of holy grain,
   And this is grief to me.

JOHN PEALE BISHOP

THE FISH

I caught a tremendous fish
and held him beside the boat
half out of water, with my hook
fast in a corner of his mouth.
He didn't fight.
He hadn't fought at all.
He hung a grunting weight,
battered and venerable
and homely. Here and there
his brown skin hung in strips
like ancient wall-paper,
and its pattern of darker brown

was like wall-paper:
shapes like full-blown roses
stained and lost through age.
He was speckled with barnacles,
fine rosettes of lime,
and infested
with tiny white sea-lice,
and underneath two or three
rags of green weed hung down.
While his gills were breathing in
the terrible oxygen
—the frightening gills,
fresh and crisp with blood,
that can cut so badly—
I thought of the coarse white flesh
packed in like feathers,
the big bones and the little bones,
the dramatic reds and blacks
of his shiny entrails,
and the pink swim-bladder
like a big peony.
I looked into his eyes
which were far larger than mine
but shallower, and yellowed,
the irises backed and packed
with tarnished tinfoil
seen through the lenses
of old scratched isinglass.
They shifted a little, but not

to return my stare.
—It was more like the tipping
of an object toward the light.
I admired his sullen face,
the mechanism of his jaw,
and then I saw
that from his lower lip
—if you could call it a lip—
grim, wet, and weapon-like,
hung five old pieces of fish-line,
or four and a wire leader
with the swivel still attached,
with all their five big hooks
grown firmly in his mouth.
A green line, frayed at the end
where he broke it, two heavier lines
and a fine black thread
still crimped from the strain and snap
when it broke and he got away.
Like medals with their ribbons
frayed and wavering,
a five-haired beard of wisdom
trailing from his aching jaw.
I stared and stared
and victory filled up
the little rented boat,
from the pool of bilge
where oil had spread a rainbow
around the rusted engine,

to the bailer rusted orange,
the sun-cracked thwarts,
the oarlocks on their strings,
the gunnels—until everything
was rainbow, rainbow, rainbow!
And I let the fish go.

ELIZABETH BISHOP

TO DAFFADILLS

1. Faire Daffadills, we weep to see
    You haste away so soone:
   As yet the early-rising Sun
    Has not attain'd his Noone.
     Stay, stay,
      Untill the hasting day
       Has run
      But to the Even-song;
   And, having pray'd together, we
      Will goe with you along.

2. We have short time to stay, as you,
    We have as short a Spring;
   As quick a growth to meet Decay,
    As you, or any thing.
     We die,
      As your hours doe, and drie

>   Away,
>   Like to the Summers raine;
>   Or as the pearles of Mornings dew
>   Ne'r to be found againe.

ROBERT HERRICK

DAFFODILS

I wandered lonely as a cloud
   That floats on high o'er vales and hills,
When all at once I saw a crowd,
   A host, of golden daffodils,
Beside the lake, beneath the trees,
Fluttering, dancing in the breeze.

Continuous as the stars that shine
   And twinkle on the Milky Way,
They stretched in never-ending line
   Along the margin of a bay:
Ten thousand saw I at a glance,
Tossing their heads in sprightly dance.

The waves beside them danced, but they
   Outdid the sparkling waves in glee;
A poet could not but be gay
   In such a jocund company;
I gazed, and gazed, but little thought
What wealth the show to me had brought:

For oft, when on my couch I lie,
    In vacant or in pensive mood,
They flash upon that inward eye
    Which is the bliss of solitude;
And then my heart with pleasure fills,
And dances with the daffodils.

WILLIAM WORDSWORTH

THE RUNAWAY

Once when the snow of the year was beginning to fall,
We stopped by a mountain pasture to say, "Whose colt?"
A little Morgan had one forefoot on the wall,
The other curled at his breast. He dipped his head
And snorted to us. And then he had to bolt.
We heard the miniature thunder where he fled,
And we saw him, or thought we saw him, dim and gray,
Like a shadow against the curtain of falling flakes.
"I think the little fellow's afraid of the snow.
He isn't winter-broken. It isn't play
With the little fellow at all. He's running away.
I doubt if even his mother could tell him, 'Sakes,
It's only weather.' He'd think she didn't know!
Where is his mother? He can't be out alone."
And now he comes again with a clatter of stone
And mounts the wall again with whited eyes
And all his tail that isn't hair up straight.
He shudders his coat as if to throw off flies.

"Whoever it is that leaves him out so late,
When other creatures have gone to stall and bin,
Ought to be told to come and take him in."

ROBERT FROST

SONG—THE OWL

I

When cats run home and light is come,
   And dew is cold upon the ground,
And the far-off stream is dumb,
   And the whirring sail goes round,
   And the whirring sail goes round;
     Alone and warming his five wits,
     The white owl in the belfry sits.

II

When merry milkmaids click the latch,
   And rarely smells the new-mown hay,
And the cock hath sung beneath the thatch
   Twice or thrice his roundelay,
   Twice or thrice his roundelay;
     Alone and warming his five wits,
     The white owl in the belfry sits.

ALFRED, LORD TENNYSON

THE EAGLE

Fragment

He clasps the crag with crooked hands;
Close to the sun in lonely lands,
Ring'd with the azure world, he stands,

The wrinkled sea beneath him crawls;
He watches from his mountain walls,
And like a thunderbolt he falls.

ALFRED, LORD TENNYSON

TIGER LILY

The tiger lily is a panther,
Orange to black spot:
Her tongue is the velvet pretty anther,
And she's in the vacant lot.

The cool day lilies grow beside her,
But they are done now and dead,
And between them a little silver spider
Hangs from a thread.

DAVID MC CORD

THE BLACKBIRD

In the far corner
close by the swings,
every morning
a blackbird sings.

His bill's so yellow,
His coat's so black,
that he makes a fellow
whistle back.

Ann, my daughter,
thinks that he
sings for us two
especially.

HUMBERT WOLFE

CONDORS

1. CONDORS FLYING

We watched the Condors winging towards the Moon,
A Moon that glimmered in the blue daylight;
Around us were the Andes, and beyond
Andes, the Ocean, empty like the Moon.
I heard you speak in Atahualpa's tongue:

Then distances grew present; all the range
Of Condors' wings between my thought, your thought:
As though they had transcended need for wings,
We watched the Condors winging towards the Moon.

II. CONDORS IN THE JARDIN DES PLANTES

To sink into the depths we need take weights—
Put on such armour as our divers use;
To rise above the fathomed we must bear
Weights, and you are weighted for emprise
Of rising to where flows the thinnest air,
And here beneath our towers you roost and run,
And trail your wings. I think I know your pain,
Your pain and weariness!
Like divers are ye that perpetually,
Plated in metal, make circuit about
Where some sidereal gesture has withdrawn
The tides, the main—
Condors with shuttered, iron-heavy wings!

PADRAIC COLUM

THE SIX BADGERS

As I was a-hoeing, a-hoeing my lands
Six badgers came up with white wands in their hands.
They made a ring around me and, bowing, they said:
"Hurry home, Farmer George, for the table is spread!

There's pie in the oven, there's beef on the plate:
Hurry home, Farmer George, if you would not be late!"
So homeward I went, but could not understand
Why six fine dog-badgers with white wands in hand
Should seek me out hoeing and bow in a ring,
And all to inform me so common a thing!

ROBERT GRAVES

A BIRD CAME DOWN THE WALK

A bird came down the walk:
He did not know I saw;
He bit an angle-worm in halves
And ate the fellow, raw.

And then he drank a dew
From a convenient grass,
And then hopped sidewise to the wall
To let a beetle pass.

He glanced with rapid eyes
That hurried all abroad,—
They looked like frightened beads, I thought
He stirred his velvet head

Like one in danger; cautious,
I offered him a crumb,
And he unrolled his feathers
And rowed him softer home

Than oars divide the ocean,
Too silver for a seam,
Or butterflies, off banks of noon,
Leap, plashless, as they swim.

EMILY DICKINSON

FIREFLY

A Song

A little light is going by,
Is going up to see the sky,
A little light with wings.

I never could have thought of it,
To have a little bug all lit
And made to go on wings.

ELIZABETH MADOX ROBERTS

ENVOI

Fly, white butterflies, out to sea,
Frail pale wings for the wind to try,
Small white wings that we scarce can see,
   Fly.

Some fly light as a laugh of glee,
Some fly soft as a low long sigh:
All to the haven where each would be,
   Fly.

ALGERNON CHARLES SWINBURNE

THE LITTLE TURTLE

There was a little turtle.
He lived in a box.
He swam in a puddle.
He climbed on the rocks.

He snapped at a mosquito.
He snapped at a flea.
He snapped at a minnow.
And he snapped at me.

He caught the mosquito.
He caught the flea.
He caught the minnow.
But he didn't catch me.

VACHEL LINDSAY

THE BAT

By day the bat is cousin to the mouse.
He likes the attic of an ageing house.

His fingers make a hat about his head.
His pulse beat is so slow we think him dead.

He loops in crazy figures half the night
Among the trees that face the corner light.

But when he brushes up against a screen,
We are afraid of what our eyes have seen:

For something is amiss or out of place
When mice with wings can wear a human face.

THEODORE ROETHKE

DAHLIAS

When we behold
Flowers of the magnitude of these,
We dream the gardens that were Atlas's
Before the pride of his descendants made
Atlantis but a name. Dahlias
Beside the nettle-green of Autumn gardens,
    Yellow as masks of gold,
Dark-red like wine the Sea-kings pour from galleys,
And pink as clouds the early oarsman
Above bright Ophir and dark Gades sees.

PADRAIC COLUM

ALLIE

Allie, call the birds in,
    The birds from the sky!
Allie calls, Allie sings;
    Down they all fly:
First there came
Two white doves,
    Then a sparrow from his nest
Then a clucking bantam hen
    Then a robin red-breast.

Allie, call the beasts in,
    The beasts, every one!
Allie calls, Allie sings,
    In they all run:
First there came
Two black lambs,
    Then a grunting Berkshire sow,
Then a dog without a tail,
    Then a red and white cow.

Allie, call the fish up,
    The fish from the stream!
Allie calls, Allie sings,
    Up they all swim:
First there came
Two gold fish,
    A minnow and a miller's thumb
Then a school of little trout,
    Then the twisting eels come.

Allie, call the children,
    Call them from the green!
Allie calls, Allie sings,
    Soon they run in:
First there came
Tom and Madge,
    Kate and I who'll not forget

How we played by the water's edge
    Till the April sun set.

ROBERT GRAVES

I HAVE LOVED FLOWERS

I have loved flowers that fade,
Within whose magic tents
Rich hues have marriage made
With sweet unmemoried scents:
A honeymoon delight,—
A joy of love at sight,
That ages in an hour:—
My song be like a flower!

I have loved airs that die
Before their charm is writ
Along a liquid sky
Trembling to welcome it.
Notes that with pulse of fire
Proclaim the spirit's desire,
Then die, and are nowhere:—
My song be like an air!

Die, song, die like a breath,
And wither as a bloom:
Fear not a flowery death,
Dread not an airy tomb!

Fly with delight, fly hence!
'Twas thine love's tender sense
To feast; now on thy bier
Beauty shall shed a tear.

ROBERT BRIDGES

BAVARIAN GENTIANS

Not every man has gentians in his house
in soft September, at slow, sad Michaelmas.

Bavarian gentians, big and dark, only dark
darkening the day-time torch-like with the smoking blueness
   of Pluto's gloom,
ribbed and torch-like, with their blaze of darkness spread blue
down flattening into points, flattened under the sweep
   of white day
torch-flower of the blue-smoking darkness, Pluto's dark-blue daze,
black lamps from the halls of Dis, burning dark blue,
giving off darkness, blue darkness, as Demeter's pale lamps
   give off light,
lead me then, lead me the way.

Reach me a gentian, give me a torch!
let me guide myself with the blue, forked torch of this flower
down the darker and darker stairs, where blue is darkened
   on blueness,

even where Persephone goes, just now, from the frosted September
to the sightless realm where darkness is awake upon the dark
and Persephone herself is but a voice
or a darkness invisible enfolded in the deeper dark
of the arms Plutonic, and pierced with the passion
    of dense gloom,
among the splendor of torches of darkness, shedding darkness
    on the lost bride and her groom.

D. H. LAWRENCE

SNAIL

Snail upon the wall,
Have you got at all
Anything to tell
About your shell?

Only this, my child—
When the wind is wild,
Or when the sun is hot,
It's all I've got.

JOHN DRINKWATER

FLOWERS BY THE SEA

When over the flowery, sharp pasture's
edge, unseen, the salt ocean

lifts its form—chickory and daisies
tied, released, seem hardly flowers alone

but color and the movement—or the shape
perhaps—of restlessness, whereas

the sea is circled and sways
peacefully upon its plantlike stem

WILLIAM CARLOS WILLIAMS

ADLESTROP

Yes, I remember Adlestrop—
The name, because one afternoon
Of heat the express-train drew up there
Unwontedly. It was late June.

The stream hissed. Someone cleared his throat.
No one left and no one came
On the bare platform. What I saw
Was Adlestrop—only the name

And willows, willow-herb, and grass,
And meadowsweet, and haycocks dry,
No whit less still and lonely fair
Than the high cloudlets in the sky.

And for that minute a blackbird sang
Close by, and round him, mistier,
Farther and farther, all the birds
Of Oxfordshire and Gloucestershire.

EDWARD THOMAS

THEIR LONELY BETTERS

As I listened from a beach-chair in the shade
To all the noises that my garden made,
It seemed to me only proper that words
Should be withheld from vegetables and birds.

A robin with no Christian name ran through
The Robin-Anthem which was all it knew,
And rustling flowers for some third party waited
To say which pairs, if any, should get mated.

No one of them was capable of lying,
There was not one which knew that it was dying
Or could have with a rhythm or a rhyme
Assumed responsibility for time.

Let them leave language to their lonely betters
Who count some days and long for certain letters;
We, too, make noises when we laugh or weep,
Words are for those with promises to keep.

W. H. AUDEN

ZEBRA

The eagle's shadow runs across the plain,
Towards the distant, nameless, air-blue mountains.
But the shadows of the round young Zebra
Sit close between their delicate hoofs all day,
    where they stand immovable,
And wait for the evening, wait to stretch out, blue,
Upon a plain, painted brick-red by the sunset,
And to wander to the water-hole.

ISAK DINESEN

THE MYSTERIOUS CAT

I saw a proud, mysterious cat
I saw a proud, mysterious cat,
Too proud to catch a mouse or rat—
Mew, mew, mew.

But catnip she would eat, and purr,
But catnip she would eat, and purr.
And goldfish she did much prefer—
Mew, mew, mew.

I saw a cat—'twas but a dream,
I saw a cat—'twas but a dream
Who scorned the slave that brought her cream—
Mew, mew, mew.

Unless the slave were dressed in style,
Unless the slave were dressed in style
And knelt before her all the while—
Mew, mew, mew.

Did you ever hear of a thing like that?
Did you ever hear of a thing like that?
Did you ever hear of a thing like that?
Oh, what a proud mysterious cat.
Oh, what a proud mysterious cat.
Oh, what a proud mysterious cat.
Mew . . . Mew . . . Mew.

VACHEL LINDSAY

DOG

Dogs are quite a bit like people,
   Or so it seems to me somehow.
Like people, Dogs go anywhere,
They swim in the sea, they leap through the air,
They bark and growl, they sit and stare,
They even wear what people wear.
Look at that Poodle with a hat on its noodle,
Look at that Boxer in a long silver-fox fur,
Look at that Whippet in its calico tippet,
Look at that Sealyham in diamonds from Rotterdam,
Look at that Afghan wrapped in an afghan,
Look at that Chow down there on a dhow
All decked out for some big powwow
With Pekinese waiting to come kowtow.
   Don't they all look just like people?
   People you've *seen* somewhere? Bowwow!

WILLIAM JAY SMITH

THE CATERPILLAR

Brown and furry
Caterpillar in a hurry,
Take your walk
To the shady leaf, or stalk,
   Or what not,

Which may be the chosen spot.
   No toad spy you,
Hovering bird of prey pass by you;
Spin and die,
To live again as butterfly.

CHRISTINA ROSSETTI

THE THRUSH'S NEST

Within a thick and spreading hawthorn bush,
That overhung a molehill large and round,
I heard from morn to morn a merry thrush
Sing hymns to sunrise, and I drank the sound
With joy; and often, an intruding guest,
I watched her secret toil from day to day
How true she warped the moss, to form a nest,
And modelled it within with wood and clay;
And by-and-by, like heath bells gilt with dew,
There lay her shining eggs, as bright as flowers,
Ink-spotted over shells of greeny blue;
And there I witnessed in the sunny hours,
A brood of Nature's minstrels chirp and fly,
Glad as the sunshine and the laughing sky.

JOHN CLARE

BUTTERFLY

Of living creatures most I prize
Black-spotted yellow Butterflies
Sailing softly through the skies,

Whisking light from each sunbeam,
Gliding over field and stream—
Like fans unfolding in a dream,

Like fans of gold lace flickering
Before a drowsy elfin king
For whom the thrush and linnet sing—

Soft and beautiful and bright
As hands that move to touch the light
When Mother leans to say good night.

WILLIAM JAY SMITH

SPRING AND SUMMER

WRITTEN IN MARCH

The Cock is crowing,
The stream is flowing,
The small birds twitter,
The lake doth glitter,
The green field sleeps in the sun;
The oldest and youngest
Are at work with the strongest;
The cattle are grazing,
Their heads never raising;
There are forty feeding like one!
Like an army defeated
The snow hath retreated,
And now doth fare ill
On the top of the bare hill;
The ploughboy is whooping—anon—anon:
There's joy in the mountains;
There's life in the fountains;
Small clouds are sailing,
Blue sky prevailing;
The rain is over and gone!

WILLIAM WORDSWORTH

A WOOD SONG

Now one and all, you Roses,
    Wake up, you lie too long!
This very morning closes
    The Nightingale his song;

Each from its olive chamber
    His babies every one
This very morning clamber
    Into the shining sun.

You Slug-a-beds and Simples,
    Why will you so delay!
Dears, doff your olive wimples,
    And listen while you may.

        RALPH HODGSON

PIPPA'S SONG

The year's at the Spring,
And day's at the morn;
Morning's at seven;
The hill-side's dew-pearled;
The lark's on the wing;
The snail's on the thorn;

God's in His heaven—
All's right with the world.

ROBERT BROWNING

THE BLOSSOM

Merry, Merry Sparrow!
Under leaves so green
A happy Blossom
Sees you swift as arrow
Seek your cradle narrow
Near my Bosom.

Pretty, Pretty Robin!
Under leaves so green
A happy Blossom
Hears you sobbing, sobbing,
Pretty, Pretty Robin,
Near my Bosom.

WILLIAM BLAKE

COUNTRY SUMMER

Now the rich cherry, whose sleek wood,
And top with silver petals traced
Like a strict box its gems encased,
Has spilt from out that cunning lid,
All in an innocent green round,
Those melting rubies which it hid;
With moss ripe-strawberry-encrusted,
So birds get half, and minds lapse merry
To taste that deep-red, lark's-bite berry,
And blackcap bloom is yellow-dusted.

The wren that thieved it in the eaves
A trailer of the rose could catch
To her poor droopy sloven thatch,
And side by side with the wren's brood—
O lovely time of beggar's luck—
Opens the quaint and hairy bud;
And full and golden is the yield
Of cows that never have to house,
But all night nibble under boughs,
Or cool their sides in the moist field.

Into the rooms flow meadow airs,
The warm farm baking smell's blown round.
Inside and out, and sky and ground
Are much the same; the wishing star,
Hesperus, kind and early born,

Is risen only finger-far;
All stars stand close in summer air,
And tremble, and look mild as amber;
When wicks are lighted in the chamber,
They are like stars which settled there.

Now straightening from the flowery hay,
Down the still light the mowers look,
Or turn, because their dreaming shook,
And they waked half to other days,
When left alone in the yellow stubble
The rusty-coated mare would graze.
Yet thick the lazy dreams are born,
Another thought can come to mind,
But like the shivering of the wind,
Morning and evening in the corn.

LÉONIE ADAMS

THE RAINY SUMMER

There's much afoot in heaven and earth this year;
    The winds hunt up the sun, hunt up the moon,
Trouble the dubious dawn, hasten the drear
    Height of a threatening noon.

No breath of boughs, no breath of leaves, of fronds,
    May linger or grow warm; the trees are loud;
The forest, rooted, tosses in her bonds,
    And strains against the cloud.

No scents may pause within the garden-fold;
    The rifled flowers are cold as ocean-shells;
Bees, humming in the storm, carry their cold
    Wild honey to cold cells.

ALICE MEYNELL

BED IN SUMMER

In winter I get up at night
And dress by yellow candle-light.
In summer, quite the other way,
I have to go to bed by day.

I have to go to bed and see
The birds still hopping on the tree.
Or hear the grown-up people's feet
Still going past me in the street.

And does it not seem hard to you,
When all the sky is clear and blue,
And I should like so much to play,
To have to go to bed by day?

ROBERT LOUIS STEVENSON

IN BETWEEN

ARE THE PEOPLE

THE PEOPLE

The ants are walking under the ground,
And the pigeons are flying over the steeple,
And in between are the people.

ELIZABETH MADOX ROBERTS

FOREIGN CHILDREN

Little Indian, Sioux or Crow,
   Little frosty Eskimo,
   Little Turk or Japanee,
O! don't you wish that you were me?

You have seen the scarlet trees
And the lions over seas;
You have eaten ostrich eggs,
And turned the turtles off their legs.

Such a life is very fine,
But it's not so nice as mine:
You must often, as you trod,
Have wearied not to be abroad.

You have curious things to eat,
I am fed on proper meat;
You must dwell beyond the foam,
But I am safe and live at home.

    Little Indian, Sioux or Crow,
       Little frosty Eskimo,
       Little Turk or Japanee,
    O! don't you wish that you were me?

ROBERT LOUIS STEVENSON

TO A FAT LADY SEEN FROM THE TRAIN

O why do you walk through the fields in gloves,
    Missing so much and so much?
O fat white woman whom nobody loves,
Why do you walk through the fields in gloves,
When the grass is soft as the breast of doves
    And shivering-sweet to the touch?
O why do you walk through the fields in gloves,
    Missing so much and so much.

FRANCES CORNFORD

THE SONG OF QUOODLE

They haven't got no noses,
The fallen sons of Eve;
Even the smell of roses
Is not what they supposes;
But more than mind discloses
And more than men believe.

* * *

The brilliant smell of water,
The brave smell of a stone,
The smell of dew and thunder,
The old bones buried under,
Are things in which they blunder
And err, if left alone.

The wind from winter forests,
The scent of scentless flowers,
The breath of brides' adorning,
The smell of snare and warning,
The smell of Sunday morning,
God gave to us for ours.

* * *

And Quoodle here discloses
All things that Quoodle can,
They haven't got no noses,
They haven't got no noses,

And goodness only knowses
The Noselessness of Man.

G. K. CHESTERTON

THE SONG OF MR. TOAD

The world has held great Heroes,
    As history books have showed;
But never a name to go down to fame
    Compared with that of Toad!

The clever men at Oxford
    Know all that there is to be knowed.
But they none of them knew one half as much
    As intelligent Mr. Toad!

The animals sat in the Ark and cried,
    Their tears in torrents flowed.
Who was it said, "There's land ahead"?
    Encouraging Mr. Toad!

The Army all saluted
    As they marched along the road.
Was it the King? Or Kitchener?
    No. It was Mr. Toad!

The Queen and her Ladies-in-waiting
   Sat at the window and sewed.
She cried, "Look! who's that *handsome* man?"
   They answered, "Mr. Toad."

KENNETH GRAHAME

HIS CAVALIER

Give me that man, that dares bestride
The active Sea-horse, & with pride,
Through that huge field of waters ride:
Who, with his looks too, can appease
The ruffling winds and raging Seas,
In mid'st of all their outrages.
This, this a virtuous man can doe,
Saile against Rocks, and split them too;
I! and a world of Pikes passe through.

ROBERT HERRICK

TO MISTRESS MARGARET HUSSEY

Merry Margaret,
As midsummer flower,
Gentle as falcon
Or hawk of the tower;

With solace and gladness,
Much mirth and no madness,
All good and no badness,
So joyously
So maidenly,
So womanly
Her demeaning
In every thing,
Far, far passing
That I can endite,
Or suffice to write
Of merry Margaret
As midsummer flower,
Gentle as falcon
Or hawk of the tower;
   As patient and as still,
And as full of good will,
As fair Ysaphill;
Coliaunder,
Sweet pomaunder,
Good Cassaunder;
Steadfast of thought,
Well made, well wrought;
Far may be sought
Erst that ye can find
So courteous, so kind
As merry Margaret,
This midsummer flower,

Gentle as falcon
Or hawk of the tower.

JOHN SKELTON

coliaunder; *coriander*
pomaunder; *perfume-box*
erst; *before*

THE PURIST

I give you now Professor Twist,
A conscientious scientist.
Trustees exclaimed, "He never bungles!"
And sent him off to distant jungles.
Camped on a tropic riverside,
One day he missed his loving bride.
She had, the guide informed him later,
Been eaten by an alligator.
Professor Twist could not but smile.
"You mean," he said, " a crocodile."

OGDEN NASH

SARAH BYNG

WHO COULD NOT READ AND WAS TOSSED INTO A THORNY HEDGE BY A BULL

Some years ago you heard me sing
My doubts on Alexander Byng.
His sister Sarah now inspires
My jaded Muse, my failing fires.
Of Sarah Byng the tale is told
How when the child was twelve years old
She could not read or write a line.

Her sister Jane, though barely nine,
Could spout the Catechism through
And parts of Matthew Arnold too,
While little Bill
          who came between
Was quite unnaturally keen
      On
          "Athalie," by Jean Racine.

But not so Sarah! Not so Sal!
She was a most uncultured girl
Who didn't care a pinch of snuff
For any literary stuff
And gave the classics all a miss.
Observe the consequence of this!
As she was walking home one day,
Upon the fields across her way

A gate, securely padlocked, stood,
And by its side a piece of wood
On which was painted plain and full,

BEWARE THE VERY
FURIOUS BULL.

Alas! The young illiterate
Went blindly forward to her fate,
And ignorantly climbed the gate!

Now happily the Bull that day
Was rather in the mood for play
Than goring people through and through
As Bulls so very often do;
He tossed her lightly with his horns
Into a prickly hedge of thorns,
And stood by laughing while she strode
And pushed and struggled to the road.

The lesson was not lost upon
The child, who since has always gone
A long way round to keep away
From signs, whatever they may say,
And leaves a padlocked gate alone.
Moreover she has wisely grown
Confirmed in her instinctive guess
That literature breeds distress.

HILAIRE BELLOC

THE STORY OF AUGUSTUS
WHO WOULD NOT HAVE ANY SOUP

Augustus was a chubby lad;
Fat, ruddy cheeks Augustus had;
And everybody saw with joy
The plump and hearty, healthy boy.
He ate and drank as he was told,
And never let his soup get cold.

But one day, one cold winter's day,
He screamed out: "Take that soup away!
O take the nasty soup away!
I won't have any soup to-day."

Next day begins his tale of woes;
Quite lank and lean Augustus grows.
Yet, though he feels so weak and ill,
The naughty fellow cries out still—
"Not any soup for me, I say:
O take the nasty soup away!
I won't have any soup today."

The third day comes; O what a sin!
To make himself so pale and thin.
Yet, when the soup is put on table,
He screams, as loud as he is able,
"Not any soup for me, I say:
O take the nasty soup away!
I won't have any soup to-day."

Look at him, now the fourth day's come!
He scarcely weighs a sugar-plum;
He's like a little bit of thread,
And on the fifth day, he was—dead!

HEINRICH HOFFMANN

LOOK, EDWIN!

Look, Edwin! Do you see that boy
Talking to that other boy?
No, over there by those two men—
Wait, don't look now—now look again.
No, not the one in navy-blue;
That's the one he's talking to.
Sure you see him? Stripèd pants?
Well, *he was born in Paris, France.*

EDNA ST. VINCENT MILLAY

GO, LOVELY ROSE

Love Poems

AN IMMORALITY

Sing we for love and idleness,
Naught else is worth the having.

Though I have been in many a land,
There is naught else in living.

And I would rather have my sweet,
Though rose-leaves die of grieving,

Than do high deeds in Hungary
To pass all men's believing.

                EZRA POUND

WILL YOU COME?

Will you come?
Will you come?
Will you ride
So late
At my side?
O, will you come?

Will you come?
Will you come
If the night
Has a moon,
Full and bright?
O, will you come?

Would you come?
Would you come
If the noon
Gave light,
Not the moon?
Beautiful, would you come?

Would you have come?
Would you have come
Without scorning,
Had it been
Still morning?
Beloved, would you have come?

If you come
Haste and come.
Owls have cried;
It grows dark
To ride.
Beloved, beautiful, come.

EDWARD THOMAS

ALL IN GREEN WENT MY LOVE RIDING

All in green went my love riding
on a great horse of gold
into the silver dawn.

four lean hounds crouched low and smiling
the merry deer ran before.

Fleeter be they than dappled dreams
the swift sweet deer
the red rare deer.

Four red roebuck at a white water
the cruel bugle sang before.

Horn at hip went my love riding
riding the echo down
into the silver dawn.

four lean hounds crouched low and smiling
the level meadows ran before.

Softer be they than slippered sleep
the lean lithe deer
the fleet flown deer.

Four fleet does at a gold valley
the famished arrow sang before.

Bow at belt went my love riding
riding the mountain down
into the silver dawn.

four lean hounds crouched low and smiling
the sheer peaks ran before.

Paler be they than daunting death
the sleek slim deer
the tall tense deer.

Four tall stags at a green mountain
the lucky hunter sang before.

All in green went my love riding
on a great horse of gold
into the silver dawn.

four lean hounds crouched low and smiling
my heart fell dead before.

E. E. CUMMINGS

PORTRAIT OF A GIRL

This is the shape of the leaf, and this of the flower,
And this the pale bole of the tree
Which watches its bough in a pool of unwavering water
In a land we never shall see.

The thrush on the bough is silent, the dew falls softly,
In the evening is hardly a sound. . . .
And the three beautiful pilgrims who come here together
Touch lightly the dust of the ground.

Touch it with feet that trouble the dust but as wings do,
Come shyly together, are still,
Like dancers who wait in a pause of the music, for music
The exquisite silence to fill . . .

This is the thought of the first, and this of the second,
And this the grave thought of the third:
"Linger we thus for a moment, palely expectant,
And silence will end, and the bird

"Sing the pure phrase, sweet phrase, clear phrase in the twilight
To fill the blue bell of the world;
And we, who on music so leaflike have drifted together,
Leaflike apart shall be whirled

"Into what but the beauty of silence, silence forever? . . ."
. . . This is the shape of the tree,
And the flower and the leaf, and the three pale beautiful pilgrims:
This is what you are to me.

CONRAD AIKEN

A PAVANE FOR THE NURSERY

Now touch the air softly,
Step gently. One, two . . .
I'll love you till roses
Are robin's-egg blue;
I'll love you till gravel
Is eaten for bread,
And lemons are orange,
And lavender's red.

Now touch the air softly,
Swing gently the broom.
I'll love you till windows
Are all of a room;
And the table is laid,
And the table is bare,

And the ceiling reposes
On bottomless air.

I'll love you till Heaven
Rips the stars from his coat,
And the Moon rows away in
A glass-bottomed boat;
And Orion steps down
Like a diver below,
And Earth is ablaze,
And Ocean aglow.

So touch the air softly,
And swing the broom high.
We will dust the gray mountains,
And sweep the blue sky;
And I'll love you as long
As the furrow the plow,
As However is Ever,
And Ever is Now.

WILLIAM JAY SMITH

THERE IS A GARDEN IN HER FACE

There is a garden in her face
    Where roses and white lilies grow;
A heavenly paradise is that place
    Wherein all pleasant fruits do flow.

There cherries grow which none may buy,
Till "cherry-ripe" themselves do cry.

Those cherries fairly do enclose
    Of orient pearl a double row,
Which when her lovely laughter shows,
    They look like rosebuds filled with snow.
Yet them no peer nor prince can buy,
Till "cherry-ripe" themselves do cry.

Her eyes like angels watch them still,
    Her brows like bended bows do stand,
Threatening with piercing frowns to kill
    All that attempt, with eye or hand,
Those sacred cherries to come nigh,
Till "cherry-ripe" themselves do cry.

THOMAS CAMPION

STILLNESS

When the words rustle no more,
    And the last work's done,
When the bolt lies deep in the door,
    And Fire, our Sun,
Falls on the dark-laned meadows of the floor;

When the clock's last chime to the next chime
    Silence beats his drum,
And Space with gaunt grey eyes and her brother Time
    Wheeling and whispering come,
She with the mould of form and he with the loom of rhyme:

Then twittering out in the night my thought-birds flee,
    I am emptied of all my dreams:
I only hear Earth turning, only see
    Ether's long bankless streams,
And only know I should drown if you laid not your hand on me.

JAMES ELROY FLECKER

A SONG

With Love among the haycocks
We played at hide and seek;

He shut his eyes and counted—
    We hid among the hay—
Then he a haycock mounted,
    And spied us where we lay;

And O! the merry laughter
Across the hayfield after!

RALPH HODGSON

SONG

Go, lovely Rose—
Tell her that wastes her time and me,
That now she knows,
When I resemble her to thee,
How sweet and fair she seems to be.

Tell her that's young,
And shuns to have her graces spied,
That hadst thou sprung
In deserts where no men abide,
Thou must have uncommended died.

Small is the worth
Of beauty from the light retired:
Bid her come forth,
Suffer herself to be desired,
And not blush so to be admired.

Then die—that she
The common fate of all things rare
May read in thee;
How small a part of time they share
That are so wondrous sweet and fair!

EDMUND WALLER

MANY LOVE MUSIC

INTRODUCTION

Piping down the valleys wild,
Piping songs of pleasant glee,
On a cloud I saw a child,
And he laughing said to me:

"Pipe a song about a Lamb!"
So I piped with merry chear.
"Piper, pipe that song again;"
So I piped: he wept to hear.

"Drop thy pipe, thy happy pipe;
"Sing thy songs of happy chear:"
So I sung the same again,
While he wept with joy to hear.

"Piper, sit thee down and write
"In a book, that all may read."
So he vanish'd from my sight,
And I pluck'd a hollow reed,

And I made a rural pen,
And I stain'd the water clear,
And I wrote my happy songs
Every child may joy to hear.

WILLIAM BLAKE

INFANT JOY

"I have no name:
"I am but two days old."
What shall I call thee?
"I happy am,
"Joy is my name."
Sweet joy befall thee!

Pretty joy!
Sweet joy but two days old,
Sweet joy I call thee:
Thou dost smile,
I sing the while,
Sweet joy befall thee!

WILLIAM BLAKE

MUSICIAN

Where have these hands been,
By what delayed,
That so long stayed
Apart from the thin

Strings which they now grace
With their lonely skill?
Music and their cool will
At last interlace.

Now with great ease, and slow,
The thumb, the finger, the strong
Delicate hand plucks the long
String it was born to know.

And, under the palm, the string
Sings as it wished to sing.

LOUISE BOGAN

TO MUSIQUE, TO BECALME HIS FEVER

1. Charm me asleep, and melt me so
    With thy Delicious Numbers;
  That being ravisht, hence I goe
    Away in easie slumbers.
      Ease my sick head,
      And make my bed,
    Thou Power that canst sever
      From me this ill:
      And quickly still:
      Though thou not kill
        My Fever.

133

2. Thou sweetly canst convert the same
      From a consuming fire,
   Into a gentle-licking flame,
      And make it thus expire.
       Then make me weep
       My paines asleep;
   And give me such reposes,
       That I, poore I,
       May think, thereby,
       I live and die
         'Mongst Roses.

3. Fall on me like a silent dew,
      Or like those Maiden showrs,
   Which, by the peepe of day, doe strew
      A Baptime o're the flowers.
       Melt, melt my paines,
       With thy soft straines;
   That having ease me given,
       With full delight,
       I leave this light;
       And take my flight
         For Heaven.

ROBERT HERRICK

THERE'D BE AN ORCHESTRA

From "Thousand-and-First Ship"

> There'd be an orchestra
>   Bingo! Bango!
> Playing for us
>   To dance the tango,
> And people would clap
>   When we arose,
> At her sweet face
>   And my new clothes.

F. SCOTT FITZGERALD

WHO GOES WITH FERGUS?

Who will go drive with Fergus now,
And pierce the deep wood's woven shade,
And dance upon the level shore?
Young man, lift up your russet brow,
And lift your tender eyelids, maid,
And brood on hopes and fear no more.

And no more turn aside and brood
Upon love's bitter mystery:
For Fergus rules the brazen cars,
And rules the shadows of the wood,

And the white breast of the dim sea
And all dishevelled wandering stars.

W. B. YEATS

THE SONG OF THE MAD PRINCE

Who said, "Peacock Pie"?
   The old King to the sparrow:
Who said, "Crops are ripe"?
   Rust to the harrow:
Who said, "Where sleeps she now?
   Where rests she now her head,
Bathed in eve's loveliness"? —
   That's what I said.

Who said, "Ay, mum's the word";
   Sexton to willow:
Who said, "Green dusk for dreams,
   Moss for a pillow"?
Who said, "All Time's delight
   Hath she for narrow bed;
Life's troubled bubble broken"? —
   That's what I said.

WALTER DE LA MARE

THE DANCE

In Breughel's great picture, The Kermess,
the dancers go round, they go round and
around, the squeal and the blare and the
tweedle of bagpipes, a bugle and fiddles
tipping their bellies (round as the thick-
sided glasses whose wash they impound)
their hips and their bellies off balance
to turn them. Kicking and rolling about
the Fair Grounds, swinging their butts, those
shanks must be sound to bear up under such
rollicking measures, prance as they dance
in Breughel's great picture, The Kermess.

WILLIAM CARLOS WILLIAMS

M., SINGING

Now, innocent, within the deep
Night of all things you turn the key,
Unloosing what we know in sleep.
In your fresh voice they cry aloud
Those beings without heart or name.

Those creatures both corrupt and proud,
Upon the melancholy words
And in the music's subtlety,
Leave the long harvest which they reap
In the sunk land of dust and flame
And move to space beneath our sky.

LOUISE BOGAN

ARIEL'S SONG

Come unto these yellow sands,
    And then take hands:
Curtsied when you have, and kiss'd—
    The wild waves whist;
Foot it featly here and there;
And, sweet sprites, the burthen bear.
    Hark, hark!
            Bow-wow.
    The watch-dogs bark:
            Bow-wow.
Hark, hark! I hear
The strain of strutting chanticleer
Cry, Cock-a-diddle-dow.

WILLIAM SHAKESPEARE

THE SPLENDOR FALLS ON CASTLE WALLS

The splendor falls on castle walls
    And snowy summits old in story;
The long light shakes across the lakes,
    And the wild cataract leaps in glory.
Blow, bugle, blow, set the wild echoes flying,
Blow, bugle; answer, echoes, dying, dying, dying,

O, hark, O, hear! how thin and clear,
    And thinner, clearer, farther going!
O, sweet and far from cliff and scar
    The horns of Elfland faintly blowing!
Blow, let us hear the purple glens replying,
Blow, bugle; answer, echoes, dying, dying, dying.

O love, they die in yon rich sky,
    They faint on hill or field or river;
Our echoes roll from soul to soul,
    And grow for ever and for ever.
Blow, bugle, blow, set the wild echoes flying,
And answer, echoes, answer, dying, dying, dying.

            ALFRED, LORD TENNYSON

ON MUSIC

Many love music but for music's sake,
Many because her touches can awake
Thoughts that repose within the breast half-dead,
And rise to follow where she loves to lead.
What various feelings come from days gone by!
What tears from far-off sources dim the eye!
Few, when light fingers with sweet voices play
And melodies swell, pause, and melt away,
Mind how at every touch, at every tone,
A spark of life hath glistened and hath gone.

WALTER SAVAGE LANDOR

SONG

From TWELFTH NIGHT, *Act* II, *Scene 3*

O mistress mine, where are you roaming?
O stay and hear; your true love's coming,
   That can sing both high and low:
Trip no further, pretty sweeting;
Journeys end in lovers' meeting,
   Every wise man's son doth know.

What is love? 'tis not hereafter;
Present mirth hath present laughter;
   What's to come is still unsure:
In delay there lies no plenty;
Then come and kiss me, sweet and twenty,
   Youth's a stuff will not endure.

WILLIAM SHAKESPEARE

ARIEL'S DIRGE

Full fathom five thy father lies;
   Of his bones are coral made;
Those are pearls that were his eyes;
Nothing of him that doth fade
But doth suffer a sea-change
Into something rich and strange.
Sea-nymphs hourly ring his knell:
                     Ding-dong.
Hark! now I hear them,—Ding-dong, bell.

WILLIAM SHAKESPEARE

THE SONG OF WANDERING AENGUS

I went out to the hazel wood,
Because a fire was in my head,
And cut and peeled a hazel wand,
And hooked a berry to a thread,
And when white moths were on the wing,
And moth-like stars were flickering out.
I dropped the berry in a stream
And caught a little silver trout.

When I had laid it on the floor
I went to blow the fire a-flame
But something rustled on the floor,
And someone called me by my name:
It had become a glimmering girl
With apple blossoms in her hair
Who called me by my name and ran
And faded through the brightening air.

Though I am old with wandering
Through hollow lands and hilly lands,
I will find out where she has gone,
And kiss her lips and take her hands;
And walk among long dappled grass,
And pluck till time and times are done,
The silver apples of the moon,
The golden apples of the sun.

W. B. YEATS

THEY WENT TO SEA
IN A SIEVE

Nonsense Verses

THE JUMBLIES

I

They went to sea in a Sieve, they did,
    In a Sieve they went to sea:
In spite of all their friends could say,
On a winter's morn, on a stormy day,
    In a Sieve they went to sea!
And when the Sieve turned round and round,
And every one cried, "You'll all be drowned!"
They called aloud, "Our Sieve ain't big,
But we don't care a button! we don't care a fig!
    In a Sieve we'll go to sea!"
        Far and few, far and few,
            Are the lands where the Jumblies live;
            Their heads are green, and their hands are blue,
                And they went to sea in a Sieve.

II

They sailed away in a Sieve, they did,
    In a Sieve they sailed so fast,
With only a beautiful pea-green veil
Tied with a riband by way of a sail,
    To a small tobacco-pipe mast;
And every one said, who saw them go,
"O won't they be soon upset, you know!
For the sky is dark, and the voyage is long,
And happen what may, it's extremely wrong
    In a Sieve to sail so fast!"
    Far and few, far and few,
        Are the lands where the Jumblies live;
    Their heads are green, and their hands are blue,
        And they went to sea in a Sieve.

III

The water it soon came in, it did,
    The water it soon came in;
So to keep them dry, they wrapped their feet
In a pinky paper all folded neat,
    And they fastened it down with a pin.
And they passed the night in a crockery-jar,
And each of them said, "How wise we are!
Though the sky be dark, and the voyage be long,
Yet we never can think we were rash or wrong,
    While round in our Sieve we spin!"
    Far and few, far and few,
        Are the lands where the Jumblies live;

> Their heads are green, and their hands are blue,
> And they went to sea in a Sieve.

IV

And all night long they sailed away;
    And when the sun went down,
They whistled and warbled a moony song
To the echoing sound of a coppery gong,
    In the shade of the mountains brown.
"O Timballo! How happy we are,
When we live in a sieve and a crockery-jar,
And all night long in the moonlight pale,
We sail away with a pea-green sail,
    In the shade of the mountains brown!"
> Far and few, far and few,
>   Are the lands where the Jumblies live;
> Their heads are green, and their hands are blue,
>   And they went to sea in a Sieve.

V

They sailed to the Western Sea, they did,
    To a land all covered with trees,
And they bought an Owl, and a useful Cart,
And a pound of Rice, and a Cranberry Tart,
    And a hive of silvery Bees.
And they bought a Pig, and some green Jack-daws,
And a lovely Monkey with lollipop paws,
And forty bottles of Ring-Bo-Ree,
    And no end of Stilton Cheese.

> Far and few, far and few,
>> Are the lands where the Jumblies live;
> Their heads are green, and their hands are blue,
>> And they went to sea in a Sieve.

VI

And in twenty years they all came back,
  In twenty years or more,
And every one said, "How tall they've grown!
For they've been to the Lakes, and the Torrible Zone,
  And the hills of the Chankly Bore;
And they drank their health, and gave them a feast
Of dumplings made of beautiful yeast;
And every one said, "If we only live,
We too will go to sea in a Sieve,—
  To the hills of the Chankly Bore!"
> Far and few, far and few,
>> Are the lands where the Jumblies live;
> Their heads are green, and their hands are blue,
>> And they went to sea in a Sieve.

EDWARD LEAR

JABBERWOCKY

'Twas brillig, and the slithy toves
  Did gyre and gimble in the wabe:
All mimsy were the borogoves,
  And the momeraths outgrabe.

"Beware the Jabberwock, my son!
    The jaws that bite, the claws that catch!
Beware the Jubjub bird, and shun
    The frumious Bandersnatch!"

He took his vorpal sword in hand:
    Long time the manxome foe he sought—
So rested he by the Tumtum tree,
    And stood awhile in thought.

And, as in uffish thought he stood,
    The Jabberwock, with eyes of flame,
Came whiffling through the tulgey wood,
    And burbled as it came!

One, two! One, two! And through and through
    The vorpal blade went snicker-snack!
He left it dead, and with its head
    He went galumphing back.

"And hast thou slain the Jabberwock?
    Come to my arms, my beamish boy!
O frabjous day! Callooh! Callay!"
    He chortled in his joy.

'Twas brillig, and the slithy toves
    Did gyre and gimble in the wabe:
All mimsy were the borogoves,
    And the momeraths outgrabe.

LEWIS CARROLL

JOHNNIE CRACK AND FLOSSIE SNAIL

From UNDER MILK WOOD

Johnnie Crack and Flossie Snail
Kept their baby in a milking pail
Flossie Snail and Johnnie Crack
One would pull it out and one would put it back

O it's my turn now said Flossie Snail
To take the baby from the milking pail
And it's my turn now said Johnnie Crack
To smack it on the head and put it back

Johnnie Crack and Flossie Snail
Kept their baby in a milking pail
One would put it back and one would pull it out
And all it had to drink was ale and stout
For Johnnie Crack and Flossie Snail
Always used to say that stout and ale
Was *good* for a baby in a milking pail.

DYLAN THOMAS

THE LADY AND THE BEAR

A Lady came to a Bear by a Stream.
"O why are you fishing that way?
Tell me, dear Bear there by the Stream,
Why are you fishing that way?"

"I am what is known as a Biddly Bear,—
That's why I'm fishing this way.
We Biddly's are Pee-culiar Bears.
And so,—I'm fishing this way.

And besides, it seems there's a Law:
A most, most exactious Law
Says a Bear
Doesn't dare
Doesn't dare
Doesn't DARE
Use a Hook or a Line,
Or an old piece of Twine,
Not even the end of his Claw, Claw, Claw,
Not even the end of his claw.
Yes, a Bear has to fish with his Paw, Paw.
A Bear has to fish with his Paw."

"O it's wonderful how with a flick of your Wrist,
You can fish out a fish, out a fish, out a fish,
If *I* were a fish I just couldn't resist

151

You, when you are fishing that way, that way,
When you are fishing that way."

And at that the Lady slipped from the Bank
And fell in the Stream still clutching a Plank,
But the Bear just sat there until she Sank;
As he went on fishing his way, his way,
As he went on fishing his way.

THEODORE ROETHKE

BOSTON CHARLIE

Deck us all with Boston Charlie,
  Walla Walla, Wash., an' Kalamazoo!
Nora's freezin' on the trolley,
  Swaller dollar cauliflower alley garoo!

Don't we know archaic barrel,
  Lullaby Lilla Boy, Louisville Lou.
Trolley Molly don't love Harold,
  Boola boola Pensacoola hullabaloo!

WALT KELLY

JUST DROPPED IN

Secretary of State John Foster Dulles conferred today with Burmese Premier U Nu. He said later he had come neither to woo neutral Burma nor to be wooed. . . . His reception was studiously polite.—THE NEW YORK TIMES.

He did not come to woo U Nu,
And there wasn't much of a state to-do,
And they sat around and talked, those two,
And there isn't a doubt that they mentioned Chou.

When reporters asked "A political coup?"
He waved them aside with a light "Pooh-pooh."
But he didn't just come to admire the view,
Which he certainly knew *you* knew, U Nu.

WILLIAM COLE

PETERHOF

Said Peter the Great to a Great Dane,
"Some people think I'm a little insane."
"I thought it was just that you growled when you ate,"
Said the Great Dane to Peter the Great.

EDMUND WILSON

THE SIOUX

Now what in the world shall we dioux
With the bloody and murderous Sioux
    Who some time ago
    Took an arrow and bow
And raised such a hellabelioux?

                  EUGENE FIELD

FATHER WILLIAM

"You are old, Father William," the young man said,
    "And your hair has become very white;
And yet you incessantly stand on your head—
    Do you think, at your age, it is right?"

"In my youth," Father William replied to his son,
    "I feared it might injure the brain;
But now that I'm perfectly sure I have none,
    Why, I do it again and again."

"You are old," said the youth, "as I mentioned before,
    And have grown most uncommonly fat;
Yet you turned a back somersault in at the door—
    Pray, what is the reason of that?"

"In my youth," said the sage, as he shook his gray locks,
    "I kept all my limbs very supple
By the use of this ointment—one shilling the box—
    Allow me to sell you a couple."

"You are old," said the youth, "and your jaws are too weak
    For anything tougher than suet;
Yet you finished the goose, with the bones and the beak;
    Pray, how did you manage to do it?"

"In my youth," said his father, "I took to the law,
    And argued each case with my wife;
And the muscular strength which it gave to my jaw,
    Has lasted the rest of my life."

"You are old," said the youth; "one would hardly suppose
    That your eye was as steady as ever;
Yet you balanced an eel on the end of your nose—
    What made you so awfully clever?"

"I've answered three questions, and that is enough,"
    Said his father; "don't give yourself airs!
Do you think I can listen all day to such stuff?
    Be off, or I'll kick you down-stairs!"

LEWIS CARROLL.

THE ZOBO BIRD

Do you think we skip,
Do you think we hop,
Do you think we flip,
Do you think we flop,
Do you think we trip
This fearful measure
And hop and hip
For personal pleasure?

    O no, o no,
      We are full of woe
    From top to toe:
    It's the dread Zobo,
      The Zobo bird.

He brings us bane,
He brings us blight,
He brings us pain
By day and night:
And so we must
Though it take all day
Dance or bust
Till he flies away.

    Away, away!
    O don't delay.
      Go, Zobo, go,
        O Zobo bird!

FRANK A. COLLYMORE

BALLADS

SIR PATRICK SPENS

The king sits in Dunfermlin town
    Drinking the blood-red wine;
"O where will I get a skilful skipper
    To sail this new ship of mine?"

O up and spoke an eldern* knight,
    Sat at the king's right knee;
"Sir Patrick Spens is the best sailor
    That ever sailed the sea."

The king has written a long letter,
    And sealed it with his hand,
And sent it to Sir Patrick Spens,
    Was walking on the strand.

"To Noroway, to Noroway,
    To Noroway o'er the foam;
The king's daughter o' Noroway,
    'Tis thou must bring her home."

* eldern: *olden*

The first line that Sir Patrick read
    A loud laugh laughed he;
The next line that Sir Patrick read
    The tear blinded his eye.

"O who is this has done this deed
    And told the king o' me,
To send us out, at this time of the year,
    To sail upon the sea?

"Be it wind, be it wet, be it hail, be it sleet
    Our ship must sail the foam;
The king's daughter o' Noroway,
    'Tis we must fetch her home."

They hoisted their sails on Monenday morn
    With all the speed they may;
And they have landed in Noroway
    Upon a Wodensday.

They hadna been a week, a week,
    In Noroway, but two,
When that the lords o' Noroway
    Began aloud to say,

"Ye Scottishmen spend all our king's gold,
    And a'our queen's fee!"
"Ye lie, ye lie, ye liars loud!
    For loud I hear ye lie!

"For I brought as much white money,
 As gane† my men and me,
And I brought a half-fou‡ o' good red gold,
 Out o'er the sea with me.

"Make ready, make ready, my merry men all!
 Our good ship sails the morn."
"Now ever alack, my master dear,
 I fear a deadly storm.

"I saw the new moon late yestreen§
 With the old moon in her arm;
And if we go to sea, master,
 I fear we'll come to harm."

They hadna sailed a league, a league,
 A league but barely three,
When the sky grew dark, and the wind blew loud,
 And gurly‖ grew the sea.

The anchors broke, and the topmast sprang,
 It was such a deadly storm:
And the waves came over the broken ship
 Till all her sides were torn.

---

† gane: *suffice*   ‡ half-fou: *half bushel*
§ yestreen: *yesterday*   ‖ gurly: *stormy*

"Go fetch a web of the silken cloth,
    Another of the twine,
And bind them into our ship's side,
    And let not the sea come in."

They fetched a web of the silken cloth,
    Another of the twine,
And they bound them round that good ship's side,
    But still the sea came in.

O loath, loath were our good Scots lords
    To wet their cork-heeled shoon,
But long before all the play was play'd
    They wet their hats aboon.

And many was the feather bed
    That floated on the foam,
And many was the good lord's son
    That never more came home.

O long, long, may the ladies sit,
    With their fans in their hand,
Before they see Sir Patrick Spens
    Coming sailing to the strand!

And long, long may the maidens sit
    With their gold combs in their hair,
A-waiting for their own dear loves!
    For them they'll see no more.

O forty miles off Aberdeen,
    'Tis fifty fathoms deep;
And there lies good Sir Patrick Spens,
    With the Scots lord at his feet:

ANONYMOUS

LA BELLE DAME SANS MERCI

"O what can ail thee, knight-at-arms,
    Alone and palely loitering?
The sedge has wither'd from the lake,
    And no birds sing.

"O what can ail thee, knight-at-arms,
    So haggard and so woe-begone?
The squirrel's granary is full.
    And the harvest's done.

"I see a lily on thy brow
    With anguish moist and fever-dew,
And on thy cheeks a fading rose
    Fast withereth too."

"I met a lady in the meads,
    Full beautiful—a faery's child,
Her hair was long, her foot was light,
    And her eyes were wild.

"I made a garland for her head,
    And bracelets too, and fragrant zone;*
She look'd at me as she did love,
    And made sweet moan.

"I set her on my pacing steed
    And nothing else saw all day long,
For sidelong would she bend, and sing
    A faery's song.

"She found me roots of relish sweet,
    And honey wild and manna-dew,
And sure in language strange she said
    'I love thee true.'

"She took me to her elfin grot,†
    And there she wept, and sigh'd full sore,
And there I shut her wild wild eyes
    With kisses four.

"And there she lullèd me asleep,
    And there I dream'd—Ah! woe betide!
The latest dream I ever dream'd
    On the cold hill's side.

* zone: *a belt*   † grot: *grotto*

"I saw pale kings and princes too,
     Pale warriors, death-pale were they all;
They cried—'La belle Dame sans Merci
     Hath thee in thrall!'

"I saw their starved lips in the gloam
     With horrid warning gaped wide,
And I awoke and found me here,
     On the cold hill's side.

"And this is why I sojourn here
     Alone and palely loitering,
Though the sedge is wither'd from the lake
     And no birds sing."

JOHN KEATS

THE RAVEN

Once upon a midnight dreary, while I pondered, weak and weary,
Over many a quaint and curious volume of forgotten lore—
While I nodded, nearly napping, suddenly there came a tapping,
As of some one gently rapping, rapping at my chamber door.
" 'Tis some visitor," I muttered, "tapping at my chamber door—
               Only this and nothing more."

Ah, distinctly I remember it was in the bleak December;
And each separate dying ember wrought its ghost upon the floor.

Eagerly I wished the morrow;—vainly I had sought to borrow
From my books surcease of sorrow—sorrow for the lost Lenore—
For the rare and radiant maiden whom the angels name Lenore—
>Nameless *here* for evermore.

And the silken, sad, uncertain rustling of each purple curtain
Thrilled me—filled me with fantastic terrors never felt before;
So that now, to still the beating of my heart, I stood repeating,
" 'Tis some visitor entreating entrance at my chamber door;—
>This it is and nothing more."

Presently my soul grew stronger; hesitating then no longer,
"Sir," said I, "or Madam, truly your forgiveness I implore;
But the fact is I was napping, and so gently you came rapping,
And so faintly you came tapping, tapping at my chamber door,
That I scarce was sure I heard you"—here I opened wide the door;—
>Darkness there and nothing more.

Deep into that darkness peering, long I stood there wondering, fearing,
Doubting, dreaming dreams no mortal ever dared to dream before;
But the silence was unbroken, and the stillness gave no token,
And the only word there spoken was the whispered word, "Lenore?"
This I whispered, and an echo murmured back the word "Lenore!"
>Merely this and nothing more.

Back into the chamber turning, all my soul within me burning,
Soon again I heard a tapping somewhat louder than before.
"Surely," said I, "surely that is something at my window lattice;
Let me see, then, what thereat is, and this mystery explore—
Let my heart be still a moment and this mystery explore;—
                'Tis the wind and nothing more!"

Open here I flung the shutter, when, with many a flirt and flutter,
In there stepped a stately Raven of the saintly days of yore;
Not the least obeisance made he; not a minute stopped or stayed he;
But, with mien of lord or lady, perched above my chamber door—
Perched upon a bust of Pallas just above my chamber door—
                Perched, and sat, and nothing more.

Then this ebony bird beguiling my sad fancy into smiling,
By the grave and stern decorum of the countenance it wore,
"Though thy crest be shorn and shaven, thou," I said, "art sure no craven,
Ghastly grim and ancient Raven wandering from the Nightly shore—
Tell me what thy lordly name is on the Night's Plutonian shore!"
                Quoth the Raven, "Nevermore."

Much I marvelled this ungainly fowl to hear discourse so plainly,
Though its answer little meaning—little relevancy bore;
For we cannot help agreeing that no living human being
Ever yet was blessed with seeing bird above his chamber door—

Bird or beast upon the sculptured bust above his chamber door,
                                With such name as "Nevermore."

But the Raven, sitting lonely on the placid bust, spoke only
That one word, as if his soul in that one word he did outpour.
Nothing farther then he uttered—not a feather then he fluttered—
Till I scarcely more than muttered, "Other friends have flown before—
On the morrow *he* will leave me, as my Hopes have flown before."
                                  Then the bird said, "Nevermore."

Startled at the stillness broken by reply so aptly spoken,
"Doubtless," said I, "what it utters is its only stock and store
Caught from some unhappy master whom unmerciful Disaster
Followed fast and followed faster till his songs one burden bore—
Till the dirges of his Hope that melancholy burden bore
                                  Of 'Never—nevermore.'"

But the Raven still beguiling all my fancy into smiling,
Straight I wheeled a cushioned seat in front of bird, and bust and door;
Then, upon the velvet sinking, I betook myself to linking
Fancy unto fancy, thinking what this ominous bird of yore—
What this grim, ungainly, ghastly, gaunt, and ominous bird of yore
                                  Meant in croaking "Nevermore."

This I sat engaged in guessing, but no syllable expressing
To the fowl whose fiery eyes now burned into my bosom's core;

This and more I sat divining, with my head at ease reclining
On the cushion's velvet lining that the lamp-light gloated o'er,
But whose velvet-violet lining with the lamp-light gloating o'er,
    She shall press, ah, nevermore!

Then, methought, the air grew denser, perfumed from an unseen censer
Swung by Seraphim whose foot-falls tinkled on the tufted floor.
"Wretch," I cried, "thy God hath lent thee—by these angels he hath sent thee
Respite—respite and nepenthe from thy memories of Lenore;
Quaff, oh, quaff this kind nepenthe and forget this lost Lenore!"
    Quoth the Raven, "Nevermore."

"Prophet!" said I, "thing of evil!—prophet still, if bird or devil!—
Whether Tempter sent, or whether tempest tossed thee here ashore,
Desolate yet all undaunted, on this desert land enchanted—
On this home by Horror haunted—tell me truly, I implore—
Is there—*is* there balm in Gilead?—tell me—tell me, I implore!"
    Quoth the Raven, "Nevermore."

"Prophet!" said I, "thing of evil!—prophet still, if bird or devil!
By that Heaven that bends above us—by that God we both adore—
Tell this soul with sorrow laden if, within the distant Aidenn,
It shall clasp a sainted maiden whom the angels name Lenore—
Clasp a rare and radiant maiden whom the angels name Lenore."
    Quoth the Raven, "Nevermore."

"Be that word our sign of parting, bird or fiend!" I shrieked,
    upstarting—
"Get thee back into the tempest and the Night's Plutonian shore!
Leave no black plume as a token of that lie thy soul hath spoken!
Leave my loneliness unbroken!—quit the bust above my door!
              Quoth the Raven, "Nevermore."

And the Raven, never flitting, still is sitting, *still* is sitting
On the pallid bust of Pallas just above my chamber door;
And his eyes have all the seeming of a demon's that is dreaming,
And the lamp-light o'er him streaming throws his shadow on the
    floor;
And my soul from out that shadow that lies floating on the floor
              Shall be lifted—nevermore!

EDGAR ALLAN POE

NURSERY RHYME
OF INNOCENCE AND EXPERIENCE

I had a silver penny
    And an apricot tree
And I said to the sailor
    On the white quay

"Sailor O sailor
　　Will you bring me
If I give you my penny
　　And my apricot tree

A fez from Algeria
　　An Arab drum to beat
A little gilt sword
　　And a parakeet?"

And he smiled and he kissed me
　　As strong as death
And I saw his red tongue
　　And I felt his sweet breath

"You may keep your penny
　　And your apricot tree
And I'll bring your presents
　　Back from sea."

O the ship dipped down
　　On the rim of the sky
And I waited while three
　　Long summers went by

Then one steel morning
　　On the white quay
I saw a grey ship
　　Come in from sea

Slowly she came
    Across the bay
For her flashing rigging
    Was shot away

All round her wake
    The seabirds cried
And flew in and out
    Of the hole in her side

Slowly she came
    In the path of the sun
And I heard the sound
    Of a distant gun

And a stranger came running
    Up to me
From the deck of the ship
    And he said, said he

"O are you the boy
    Who would wait on the quay
With the silver penny
    And the apricot tree?

I've a plum-coloured fez
    And a drum for thee
And a sword and a parakeet
    From over the sea."

"O where is the sailor
   With bold red hair?
And what is that volley
   On the bright air?

O where are the other
   Girls and boys?
And why have you brought me
   Children's toys?"

       CHARLES CAUSLEY

THE SEA

OREAD

Whirl up, sea—
Whirl your pointed pines.
Splash your great pines
On our rocks.
Hurl your green over us—
Cover us with your pools of fir.

H.D.

WHERE GO THE BOATS

Dark brown is the river,
    Golden is the sand.
It flows along for ever,
    With trees on either hand.

Green leaves a-floating,
    Castles of the foam,
Boats of mine a-boating—
    Where will all come home?

On goes the river
    And out past the mill,
Away down the valley,
    Away down the hill.

Away down the river,
    A hundred miles or more,
Other little children
    Shall bring my boats ashore.

ROBERT LOUIS STEVENSON

MY LOST YOUTH

Often I think of the beautiful town
    That is seated by the sea;
Often in thought go up and down
The pleasant streets of that dear old town,
    And my youth comes back to me.
        And a verse of a Lapland song
        Is haunting my memory still:
    "A boy's will is the wind's will,
And the thoughts of youth are long, long thoughts."

I can see the shadowy lines of its trees,
    And catch, in sudden gleams,
The sheen of the far-surrounding seas,
And islands that were the Hesperides

Of all my boyish dreams.
    And the burden of that old song,
    It murmurs and whispers still:
    "A boy's will is the wind's will,
And the thoughts of youth are long, long thoughts."

I remember the black wharves and the slips,
    And the sea-tides tossing free;
And Spanish sailors with bearded lips,
And the beauty and mystery of the ships,
    And the magic of the sea.
    And the voice of that wayward song
    Is singing and saying still:
    "A boy's will is the wind's will,
And the thoughts of youth are long, long thoughts."

I remember the bulwarks by the shore,
    And the fort upon the hill;
The sunrise gun, with its hollow roar,
The drum-beat repeated o'er and o'er,
    And the bugle wild and shrill.
    And the music of that old song
    Throbs in my memory still:
    "A boy's will is the wind's will,
And the thoughts of youth are long, long thoughts."

I remember the sea-fight far away,
    How it thundered o'er the tide!
And the dead captains, as they lay

In their graves, o'erlooking the tranquil bay
    Where they in battle died.
        And the sound of that mournful song
        Goes through me with a thrill:
        "A boy's will is the wind's will,
And the thoughts of youth are long, long thoughts."

I can see the breezy dome of graves,
    The shadows of Deering's Woods;
And the friendships old and the early loves
Come back with a Sabbath sound, as of doves
    In quiet neighborhoods.
        And the verse of that sweet old song,
        It flutters and murmurs still:
        "A boy's will is the wind's will,
And the thoughts of youth are long, long thoughts."

I remember the gleams and glooms that dart
    Across the school-boy's brain;
The song and the silence in the heart,
That in part are prophecies, and in part
    Are longings wild and vain.
        And the voice of that fitful song
        Sings on, and is never still:
        "A boy's will is the wind's will,
And the thoughts of youth are long, long thoughts."

There are things of which I may not speak;
    There are dreams that cannot die;

There are thoughts that make the strong heart weak,
And bring a pallor into the cheek,
   And a mist before the eye.
      And the words of that fatal song
      Come over me like a chill:
      "A boy's will is the wind's will,
And the thoughts of youth are long, long thoughts."

Strange to me now are the forms I meet
   When I visit the dear old town;
But the native air is pure and sweet,
And the trees that o'ershadow each well-known street,
   As they balance up and down,
      Are singing the beautiful song,
      Are sighing and whispering still:
      "A boy's will is the wind's will,
And the thoughts of youth are long, long thoughts."

And Deering's Woods are fresh and fair,
   And with joy that is almost pain
My heart goes back to wander there,
And among the dreams of the days that were,
   I find my lost youth again.
      And the strange and beautiful song,
      The groves are repeating it still:
      "A boy's will is the wind's will,
And the thoughts of youth are long, long thoughts."

      HENRY WADSWORTH LONGFELLOW

BREAK, BREAK, BREAK

Break, break, break
    On thy cold gray stones, O Sea!
And I would that my tongue could utter
    The thoughts that arise in me.

O well for the fisherman's boy.
    That he shouts with his sister at play!
O well for the sailor lad,
    That he sings in his boat on the bay!

And the stately ships go on
    To their haven under the hill;
But O for the touch of a vanish'd hand.
    And the sound of a voice that is still!

Break, break, break,
    At the foot of thy crags, O Sea!
But the tender grace of a day that is dead
    Will never come back to me.

            ALFRED, LORD TENNYSON

SANTORIN

(A Legend of the Aegean)

"Who are you, Sea Lady,
And where in the seas are we?
I have too long been steering
By the flashes in your eyes.
Why drops the moonlight through my heart,
And why so quietly
Go the great engines of my boat
As if their souls were free?"
"Oh ask me not, bold sailor;
Is not your ship a magic ship
That sails without a sail:
Are not these isles the Isles of Greece
And dust upon the sea?
But answer me three questions
And give me answers three.
What is your ship?" "A British."
"And where may Britain be?"
"Oh it lies north, dear lady;
It is a small country."
"Yet you will know my lover,
Though you live far away:
And you will whisper where he has gone,
That lily boy to look upon
And whiter than the spray."
"How should I know your lover,

Lady of the sea?"
"Alexander, Alexander,
The King of the World was he."
"Weep not for him, dear lady,
But come aboard my ship.
So many years ago he died,
He's dead as dead can be."
"O base and brutal sailor
To tell this lie to me.
His mother was the foam-foot
Star-sparkling Aphrodite;
His father was Adonis
Who lives away in Lebanon,
In stony Lebanon, where blooms
His red anemone.
But where is Alexander,
The soldier Alexander,
My golden love of olden days
The King of the World and me?"

She sank into the moonlight
And the sea was only sea.

JAMES ELROY FLECKER

SEE WHAT A LOVELY SHELL

See what a lovely shell.
Small and pure as a pearl,
Lying close to my foot,
Frail, but a work divine,
Made so fairily well
With delicate spire and whorl,
How exquisitely minute,
A miracle of design!

What is it? a learned man
Could give it a clumsy name.
Let him name it who can,
The beauty would be the same.

The tiny cell is forlorn,
Void of the little living will
That made it stir on the shore.
Did he stand at the diamond door
Of his house in a rainbow frill?
Did he push, when he was uncurl'd,
A golden foot or a fairy horn
Thro' his dim water-world?

Slight, to be crush'd with a tap
Of my finger-nail on the sand,
Small, but a work divine,
Frail, but a force to withstand,

Year upon year, the shock
Of cataract seas that snap
The three-decker's oaken spine
Athwart the ledges of rock,
Here on the Breton strand!

ALFRED, LORD TENNYSON

THE DARK HILLS

War Poems

THE DARK HILLS

Dark hills at evening in the west,
Where sunset hovers like a sound
Of golden horns that sang to rest
Old bones of warriors under ground,
Far now from all the bannered ways
Where flash the legions of the sun,
You fade—as if the last of days
Were fading and all wars were done.

EDWIN ARLINGTON ROBINSON

NAMING OF PARTS

Today we have naming of parts. Yesterday,
We had daily cleaning. And tomorrow morning,
We shall have what to do after firing. But today,
Today we have naming of parts. Japonica
Glistens like coral in all of the neighbouring gardens,
   And today we have naming of parts.

This is the lower sling swivel. And this
Is the upper sling swivel, whose use you will see,
When you are given your slings. And this is the piling swivel,
Which in your case you have not got. The branches
Hold in the gardens their silent, eloquent gestures,
   Which in our case we have not got.

This is the safety-catch, which is always released
With an easy flick of the thumb. And please do not let me
See anyone using his finger. You can do it quite easy
If you have any strength in your thumb. The blossoms
Are fragile and motionless, never letting anyone see
    Any of them using their finger.

And this you can see is the bolt. The purpose of this
Is to open the breech, as you see. We can slide it
Rapidly backwards and forwards; we call this
Easing the spring. And rapidly backwards and forwards
The early bees are assaulting and fumbling the flowers:
    They call it easing the Spring.

They call it easing the Spring. It is perfectly easy
If you have any strength in your thumb: like the bolt,
And the breech, and the cocking-piece, and the point of balance,
Which in our case we have not got; and the almond-blossom
Silent in all of the gardens and the bees going backwards and
    forwards,
    For today we have naming of parts.

HENRY REED

SUCCESS IS COUNTED SWEETEST

Success is counted sweetest
By those who ne'er succeed.
To comprehend a nectar
Requires sorest need.

Not one of all the purple host
Who took the flag to-day
Can tell the definition,
So clear, of victory,

As he, defeated, dying,
On whose forbidden ear
The distant strains of triumph
Burst, agonized and clear.

EMILY DICKINSON

AN IRISH AIRMAN FORESEES HIS DEATH

I know that I shall meet my fate
Somewhere among the clouds above;
Those that I fight I do not hate,
Those that I guard I do not love;
My country is Kiltartan Cross,
My countrymen Kiltartan's poor,

No likely end could bring them loss
Or leave them happier than before.
Nor law, nor duty bade me fight,
Nor public men, nor cheering crowds,
A lonely impulse of delight
Drove to this tumult in the clouds;
I balanced all, brought all to mind,
The years to come seemed waste of breath,
A waste of breath the years behind
In balance with this life, this death.

W. B. YEATS

THE TOO-LATE BORN

We too, we too, descending once again
The hills of our own land, we too have heard
 Far off—Ah, que ce cor a longue haleine—
The horn of Roland in the passages of Spain,
The first, the second blast, the failing third,
And with the third turned back and climbed once more
The steep road southward, and heard faint the sound
Of swords, of horses, the disastrous war,
And crossed the dark defile at last, and found
At Roncevaux upon the darkening plain
The dead against the dead and on the silent ground
The silent slain—

ARCHIBALD MACLEISH

FIFE TUNE

(6/8) for Sixth Platoon, 308th I.T.C.

One morning in spring
We marched from Devizes
All shapes and all sizes
Like beads on a string,
But yet with a swing
We trod the bluemetal
And full of high fettle
We started to sing.

She ran down the stair
A twelve-year-old darling
And laughing and calling
She tossed her bright hair;
Then silent to stare
At the men flowing past her—
There were all she could master
Adoring her there.

It's seldom I'll see
A sweeter or prettier;
I doubt we'll forget her
In two years or three,
And lucky he'll be
She takes for a lover
While we are far over
The treacherous sea.

JOHN MANIFOLD

ALL THAT'S PAST

CITIES AND THRONES AND POWERS

Cities and Thrones and Powers,
  Stand in Time's eye,
Almost as long as flowers,
  Which daily die;
But, as new buds put forth
  To glad new men,
Out of the spent and unconsidered Earth
  The Cities rise again.

This season's Daffodil,
  She never hears,
What change, what chance, what chill,
  Cut down last year's:
But with bold countenance,
  And knowledge small,
Esteems her seven days' continuance,
  To be perpetual.

So Time is o'er-kind,
    To all that be,
Ordains us e'en as blind,
    As bold as she:
That in our very death,
    And burial sure,
Shadow to shadow, well-persuaded, saith,
    "See how our works endure!"

RUDYARD KIPLING

THE OLD MEN ADMIRING THEMSELVES IN THE WATER

I heard the old, old men say,
"Everything alters,
And one by one we drop away."
They had hands like claws, and their knees
Were twisted like the old thorn-trees
By the waters.
I heard the old, old men say,
"All that's beautiful drifts away
Like the waters."

W. B. YEATS

INTO MY HEART

Into my heart an air that kills
    From yon far country blows:
What are those blue remembered hills,
    What spires, what farms are those?

That is the land of lost content,
    I see it shining plain:
The happy highways where I went
    And cannot come again.

A. E. HOUSMAN

A TALISMAN

Under a splintered mast,
torn from the ship and cast
    near her hull,

a stumbling shepherd found,
embedded in the ground,
    a sea-gull

of lapis lazuli,
a scarab of the sea,
    with wings spread—

>   curling its coral feet,
>   parting its beak to greet
>   men long dead.

MARIANNE MOORE

THE ROMAN ROAD

The Roman Road runs straight and bare
As the pale parting-line in hair
Across the heath. And thoughtful men
Contrast its days of Now and Then,
And delve, and measure, and compare;

Visioning on the vacant air
Helmed legionnaires, who proudly rear
The Eagle, as they pace again
> The Roman Road.

But no tall brass-helmed legionnaire
Haunts it for me. Uprises there
A mother's form upon my ken,
Guiding my infant steps, as when
We walked that ancient thoroughfare,
> The Roman Road.

THOMAS HARDY

THE MIGHTY THOUGHTS OF AN OLD WORLD

The mighty thoughts of an old world
Fan, like a dragon's wing unfurled,
  The surface of my yearnings deep;
And solemn shadows then awake,
Like the fish-lizard in the lake,
  Troubling a planet's morning sleep.

My waking is a Titan's dream,
Where a strange sun, long set, doth beam
  Through Montezuma's cypress bough:
Through the fern wilderness forlorn
Glisten the giant harts' great horn
  And serpents vast with helmed brow.

The measureless from caverns rise
With steps of earthquake, thunderous cries,
  And graze upon the lofty wood;
The palmy grove, through which doth gleam
Such antideluvian ocean's stream,
  Haunts shadowy my domestic mood.

THOMAS LOVELL BEDDOES

THE HAMMERS

Noise of hammers once I heard,
Many hammers, busy hammers,
Beating, shaping, night and day,
Shaping, beating dust and clay
To a palace; saw it reared;
Saw the hammers laid away.

And I listened, and I heard
Hammers beating, night and day,
In the palace newly reared,
Beating it to dust and clay:
Other hammers, muffled hammers,
Silent hammers of decay.

RALPH HODGSON

ALL THAT'S PAST

Very old are the woods;
    And the buds that break
Out of the brier's boughs,
    When March winds wake,
So old with their beauty are—
    Oh, no man knows
Through what wild centuries
    Roves back the rose.

Very old are the brooks;
　　And the rills that rise
Where snow sleeps cold beneath
　　The azure skies
Sing such a history
　　Of come and gone,
Their every drop is as wise
　　As Solomon.

Very old are we men;
　　Our dreams are tales
Told in dim Eden
　　By Eve's nightingales;
We wake and whisper awhile,
　　But, the day gone by,
Silence and sleep like fields
　　Of amaranth lie.

WALTER DE LA MARE

THE FLOWER-FED BUFFALOES

The flower-fed buffaloes of the spring
In the days of long ago,
Ranged where the locomotives sing
And the prairie flowers lie low;
The tossing, blooming, perfumed grass
Is swept away by wheat,

Wheels and wheels and wheels spin by
In the spring that still is sweet.
But the flower-fed buffaloes of the spring
Left us long ago.
They gore no more, they bellow no more,
They trundle around the hills no more:—
With the Blackfeet lying low,
With the Pawnees lying low.

VACHEL LINDSAY

THE HOUSE ON THE HILL

They are all gone away,
    The House is shut and still,
There is nothing more to say.

Through broken walls and gray
    The winds blow bleak and shrill;
They are all gone away.

Nor is there one today
    To speak them good or ill:
There is nothing more to say.

Why is it then we stray
    Around that sunken sill?
They are all gone away,

    And our poor fancy-play
        For them is wasted skill:
    There is nothing more to say.

EDWIN ARLINGTON ROBINSON

GONE

Where's the Queen of Sheba?
Where King Solomon?
Gone with Boy Blue who looks after the sheep,
Gone and gone and gone.

Lovely is the sunshine;
Lovely is the wheat;
Lovely the wind from out of the clouds
Having its way with it.

Rise up, Old Green-Stalks!
Delve deep, Old Corn!
But where's the Queen of Sheba?
Where King Solomon?

WALTER DE LA MARE

HERE AND NOW

LANDSCAPE AS METAL AND FLOWERS

All over America railroads ride through roses.

I should explain this is thoroughly a matter of fact.
Wherever sandy earth is piled to make a road for train tracks
The banks on either side are covered with wild, sweet
Pink rambler roses: not because roses are pretty
But because ramblers grow in cheap soil and will hold
The banks firm against rain—therefore the railroad roses.

All over America the steel-supporting flowers,
Sometimes at village depots covering the shingled station,
Sometimes embracing watertanks, but mostly endless tendrils
Out of which locomotives and pullmans flash the morning—
And tunnels the other way into whose firm, sweet evening
The whistle fades, dragging freight cars, day coaches and the
    caboose.

           WINFIELD TOWNLEY SCOTT

THE EXPRESS

After the first powerful plain manifesto
The black statement of pistons, without more fuss
But gliding like a queen, she leaves the station.
Without bowing and with restrained unconcern
She passes the houses which humbly crowd outside,
The gasworks and at last the heavy page
Of death, printed by gravestones in the cemetery.
Beyond the town there lies the open country
Where, gathering speed, she acquires mystery,
The luminous self-possession of ships on ocean.
It is now she begins to sing—at first quite low
Then loud, and at last with a jazzy madness—
The song of her whistle screaming at curves,
Of deafening tunnels, brakes, innumerable bolts.
And always light, aerial, underneath
Goes the elate metre of her wheels.
Steaming through metal landscape on her lines
She plunges new eras of wild happiness
Where speed throws up strange shapes, broad curves
And parallels clean like the steel of guns.
At last, further than Edinburgh or Rome,
Beyond the crest of the world, she reaches night
Where only a low streamline brightness
Of phosphorus on the tossing hills is white.
Ah, like a comet through flame she moves entranced

Wrapt in her music no bird song, no, nor bough
Breaking with honey buds, shall ever equal.

STEPHEN SPENDER

THIS IS JUST TO SAY

    I have eaten
    the plums
    that were in
    the icebox

    and which
    you were probably
    saving
    for breakfast

    Forgive me
    they were delicious
    so sweet
    and so cold

WILLIAM CARLOS WILLIAMS

THE BASE STEALER

Poised between going on and back, pulled
Both ways taut like a tightrope-walker,
Fingertips pointing the opposites,
Now bouncing tiptoe like a dropped ball
Or a kid skipping rope, come on, come on,
Running a scattering of steps sidewise,
How he teeters, skitters, tingles, teases,
Taunts them, hovers like an ecstatic bird,
He's only flirting, crowd him, crowd him,
Delicate, delicate, delicate, delicate—now!

ROBERT FRANCIS

ALBA

Dawn breaking as I woke,
With the white sweat of the dew
On the green, new grass.
I walked in the cold, quiet as
If it were the world beginning;
Peeling and eating a chilled tangerine.
I may have many sorrows,
Dawn is not one of them.

DEREK WALCOTT

BIG WIND

Where were the greenhouses going,
Lunging into the lashing
Wind driving water
So far down the river
All the faucets stopped?—
So we drained the manure-machine
For the steam plant,
Pumping the stale mixture
Into the rusty boilers,
Watching the pressure gauge
Waver over to red,
As the seams hissed
And the live steam
Drove to the far
End of the rose-house,
Where the worst wind was,
Creaking the cypress window-frames,
Cracking so much thin glass
We stayed all night,
Stuffing the holes with burlap;
But she rode it out,
That old rose-house,
She hove into the teeth of it,
The core and pith of that ugly storm,
Ploughing with her stiff prow,
Bucking into the wind-waves
That broke over the whole of her,

Flailing her sides with spray,
Flinging long strings of wet across the roof-top,
Finally veering, wearing themselves out, merely
Whistling thinly under the wind-vents;
She sailed until the calm morning,
Carrying her full cargo of roses.

THEODORE ROETHKE

MANHOLE COVERS

The beauty of manhole covers—what of that?
Like medals struck by a great savage khan,
Like Mayan calendar stones, unliftable, indecipherable,
Not like old electrum, chased and scored,
Mottoed and sculptured to a turn,
But notched and whelked and pocked and smashed
With the great company names:
Gentle Bethlehem, smiling United States.
This rustproof artifact of my street,
Long after roads are melted away, will lie
Sidewise in the graves of the iron-old world,
Bitten at the edges,
Strong with its cryptic American,
Its dated beauty.

KARL SHAPIRO

LYREBIRD COUNTRY

Dreams and Fancies

LYREBIRDS

Over the west side of this mountain,
that's lyrebird country.
I could go down there, they say, in the early morning,
and I'd see them, I'd hear them.

Ten years, and I have never gone.
I'll never go.
I'll never see the lyrebirds—
the few, the shy, the fabulous,
the dying poets.

I should see them, if I lay there in the dew:
first a single movement
like a waterdrop falling, then stillness,
then a brown head, brown eyes,
a splendid bird, bearing
like a crest the symbol of his art,
the high symmetrical shape of the perfect lyre.
I should hear that master practising his art.

No, I have never gone.
Some things ought to be left secret, alone;
some things—birds like walking fables—
ought to inhabit nowhere but the reverence of the heart.

JUDITH WRIGHT

THERE IS NO FRIGATE LIKE A BOOK

There is no frigate like a book
    To take us lands away,
Nor any coursers like a page
    Of prancing poetry.
This travel may the poorest take
    Without oppress of toll;
How frugal is the chariot
    That bears the human soul!

EMILY DICKINSON

AT THE BOTTOM OF THE WELL

Something befell
    Young Adam Hope,
Who had a well
    For a telescope

In which the stars
    Came crystal-clear,
Brighter than Mars
    Or Jupiter,

Till Adam scarcely
    Looked at the sky,
Strewn so sparsely,
    Stretched so high.

Night after night,
    The neighbors tell,
He put out the light,
    He stole to the well.

To that dark funnel
    He came to pray,
"If only the sun'll
    Stay away,

"And nothing occurs
    Until I finish,
One of those stars
    Will forget to vanish,

"And when that late one
    Loafs and lingers,
I'll catch a great one
    With my fingers."

Adam's aim
    Grew fixed and stronger.
Then one night came
    That lasted longer

Than nights should last
   By natural law;
And when it passed
   The neighbors saw

Something that glistened
   Deep in the well.
They looked; they listened;
   They could not tell

The tale's conclusion.
   At the end of the rope
Was it truth, or illusion,
   Or Adam Hope?

LOUIS UNTERMEYER

ROMANCE

When I was but thirteen or so
   I went into a golden land,
Chimborazo, Cotopaxi
   Took me by the hand.

My father died, my brother too,
   They passed like fleeting dreams,
I stood where Popocatapetl
   In the sunlight gleams.

I dimly heard the master's voice
    And boys far-off at play,—
Chimborazo, Cotopaxi
    Had stolen me away.

I walked in a great golden dream
    To and fro from school—
Shining Popocatapetl
    The dusty streets did rule.

I walked home with a gold dark boy
    And never a word I'd say,
Chimborazo, Cotopaxi
    Had taken my speech away.

I gazed entranced upon his face
    Fairer than any flower—
O shining Popocatapetl,
    It was thy magic hour:

The houses, people, traffic seemed
    Thin fading dreams by day;
Chimborazo, Cotopaxi
    They had stolen my soul away!

W. J. TURNER

KUBLA KHAN

In Xanadu did Kubla Khan
A stately pleasure-dome decree:
Where Alph, the sacred river, ran
Through caverns measureless to man
    Down to a sunless sea.
So twice five miles of fertile ground
With walls and towers were girdled round:
And there were gardens bright with sinuous rills,
Where blossomed many an incense-bearing tree;
And here were forests ancient as the hills,
Enfolding sunny spots of greenery.

But oh! that deep romantic chasm which slanted
Down the green hill athwart a cedarn cover!
A savage place! as holy and enchanted
As e'er beneath a waning moon was haunted
By woman wailing for her demon-lover!
And from this chasm, with ceaseless turmoil seething
As if this earth in fast thick pants were breathing,
A mighty fountain momently was forced:
Amid whose swift half-intermitted burst
Huge fragments vaulted like rebounding hail,
Or chaffy grain beneath the thresher's flail:
And 'mid these dancing rocks at once and ever
It flung up momently the sacred river.
Five miles meandering with a mazy motion
Through wood and dale the sacred river ran,

Then reached the caverns measureless to man,
And sank in tumult to a lifeless ocean:
And 'mid this tumult Kubla heard from far
Ancestral voices prophesying war!

   The shadow of the dome of pleasure
   Floated midway on the waves;
   Where was heard the mingled measure
   From the fountain and the caves.
It was a miracle of rare device,
A sunny pleasure-dome with caves of ice!

   A damsel with a dulcimer
   In a vision once I saw:
   It was an Abyssinian maid,
   And on her dulcimer she played,
   Singing of Mount Abora.
Could I revive within me
Her symphony and song,
To such a deep delight 'twould win me,
That with music loud and long,
I would build that dome in air,
That sunny dome! those caves of ice!
And all who heard should see them there,
And all should cry, Beware! Beware!
His flashing eyes, his floating hair!
Weave a circle round him thrice,
And close your eyes with holy dread,

For he on honey-dew hath fed,
And drunk the milk of Paradise.

SAMUEL TAYLOR COLERIDGE

DIGGING FOR CHINA

"Far enough down is China," somebody said.
"Dig deep enough and you might see the sky
As clear as at the bottom of a well.
Except it would be real—a different sky.
Then you could burrow down until you came
To China! Oh, it's nothing like New Jersey.
There's people, trees, and houses, and all that,
But much, much different. Nothing looks the same."

I went and got the trowel out of the shed
And sweated like a coolie all that morning,
Digging a hole beside the lilac-bush,
Down on my hands and knees. It was a sort
Of praying, I suspect. I watched my hand
Dig deep and darker, and I tried and tried
To dream a place where nothing was the same.
The trowel never did break through to blue.

Before the dream could weary of itself
My eyes were tired of looking into darkness,
My sunbaked head of hanging down a hole.

I stood up in a place I had forgotten,
Blinking and staggering while the earth went round
And showed me silver barns, the fields dozing
In palls of brightness, patens growing and gone
In the tides of leaves, and the whole sky china blue.
Until I got my balance back again
All that I saw was China, China, China.

RICHARD WILBUR

EARTHY ANECDOTE

Every time the bucks went clattering
Over Oklahoma
A firecat bristled in the way.

Wherever they went,
They went clattering,
Until they swerved
In a swift, circular line
To the right,
Because of the firecat.

Or until they swerved
In a swift, circular line
To the left,
Because of the firecat.

The bucks clattered.
The firecat went leaping,
To the right, to the left,
And
Bristled in the way.

Later, the firecat closed his bright eyes
And slept.

WALLACE STEVENS

THE SNOW MAN

One must have a mind of winter
To regard the frost and the boughs
Of the pine-trees crusted with snow;

And have been cold a long time
To behold the junipers shagged with ice,
The spruces rough in the distant glitter

Of the January sun; and not to think
Of any misery in the sound of the wind,
In the sound of a few leaves,

Which is the sound of the land
Full of the same wind
That is blowing in the same bare place

For the listener, who listens in the snow,
And, nothing himself, beholds
Nothing that is not there and the nothing that is.

WALLACE STEVENS

OVERHEARD ON A SALTMARSH

Nymph, nymph, what are your beads?

Green glass, goblin. Why do you stare at them?

Give them me.

        No.

Give them me. Give them me.

        No.

Then I will howl all night in the reeds,
Lie in the mud and howl for them.

Goblin, why do you love them so?

They are better than stars or water,
Better than voices of winds that sing,
Better than any man's fair daughter,
Your green glass beads on a silver ring.

Hush, I stole them out of the moon.

Give me your beads, I want them.

No.

I will howl in a deep lagoon
For your green glass beads, I love them so.
Give them me. Give them.

No.

HAROLD MONRO

THE GOLDEN JOURNEY TO SAMARKAND

PROLOGUE

We who with songs beguile your pilgrimage
    And swear that Beauty lives though lilies die,
We Poets of the proud old lineage
    Who sing to find your hearts, we know not why,—

What shall we tell you? Tales, marvelous tales
    Of ships and stars and isles where good men rest,
Where nevermore the rose of sunset pales,
    And winds and shadows fall toward the West:

And there the world's first huge white-bearded kings
    In dim glades sleeping, murmur in their sleep,
And closer round their breasts the ivy clings,
    Cutting its pathway slow and red and deep.

II

And how beguile you? Death has no respose
    Warmer and deeper than that Orient sand
Which hides the beauty and bright faith of those
    Who made the Golden Journey to Samarkand.

And now they wait and whiten peaceably,
    Those conquerors, those poets, those so fair:
They know time comes, not only you and I,
    But the whole world shall whiten, here or there;

When those long caravans that cross the plain
    With dauntless feet and sound of silver bells
Put forth no more for glory or for gain,
    Take no more solace from the palm-girt wells.

When the great markets by the sea shut fast
    All that calm Sunday that goes on and on:
When even lovers find their peace at last,
    And Earth is but a star, that once had shone.

JAMES ELROY FLECKER

WHEN YOU ARE OLD

WHEN YOU ARE OLD

When you are old and gray and full of sleep,
And nodding by the fire, take down this book,
And slowly read, and dream of the soft look
Your eyes had once, and of their shadows deep;

How many loved your moments of glad grace,
And loved your beauty with love false or true;
But one man loved the pilgrim soul in you,
And loved the sorrows of your changing face.

And bending down beside the glowing bars
Murmur, a little sadly, how love fled
And paced upon the mountains overhead
And hid his face amid a crowd of stars.

W. B. YEATS

SONG FROM A COUNTRY FAIR

When tunes jigged nimbler than the blood
And quick and high the bows would prance
And every fiddle string would burst
To catch what's lost beyond the string,
While half afraid their children stood,
I saw the old come out to dance.
The heart is not so light at first,
But heavy like a bough in spring.

LÉONIE ADAMS

LITTLE ELEGY

for a child who skipped rope

Here lies resting, out of breath,
Out of turns, Elizabeth
Whose quicksilver toes not quite
Cleared the whirring edge of night.

Earth whose circles round us skim
Till they catch the lightest limb,
Shelter now Elizabeth
And for her sake trip up Death.

X. J. KENNEDY

THE MIDNIGHT SKATERS

The hop-poles stand in cones,
   The icy pond lurks under,
The pole-tops touch the star-god's thrones
   And sound the gulfs of wonder,
But not the tallest there, 'tis said,
Could fathom to this pond's black bed.

Then is not Death at watch
   Within those secret waters?
What wants he but to catch
   Earth's heedless sons and daughters?
With but a crystal parapet
Between, he has his engines set.

Then on, blood shouts, on, on.
   Twirl, wheel and whip above him,
Dance on this ball-floor thin and wan,
   Use him as though you love him;
Court him, elude him, reel and pass,
And let him hate you through the glass.

EDMUND BLUNDEN

LYDIA IS GONE THIS MANY A YEAR

Lydia is gone this many a year,
    Yet when the lilacs stir,
In the old gardens far or near,
    This house is full of her.

They climb the twisted chamber stair;
    Her picture haunts the room;
On the carved shelf beneath it there,
    They heap the purple bloom.

A ghost so long has Lydia been,
    Her cloak upon the wall,
Broidered, and gilt, and faded green,
    Seems not her cloak at all.

The book, the box on mantle laid,
    The shells in a pale row,
Are those of some dim little maid,
    A thousand years ago.

And yet the house is full of her;
    She goes and comes again;
And longings thrill, and memories stir,
    Like lilacs in the rain.

Out in their yards the neighbors walk,
    Among the blossoms tall;
Of Anne, of Phyllis do they talk,
    Of Lydia not at all.

LIZETTE WOODWORTH REESE

THE GARDEN SEAT

Its former green is blue and thin,
And its once firm legs sink in and in;
Soon it will break down unaware,
Soon it will break down unaware.

At night when reddest flowers are black
Those who once sat thereon come back;
Quite a row of them sitting there,
Quite a row of them sitting there.

With them the seat does not break down,
Nor winter freeze them, nor floods drown,
For they are as light as upper air,
They are as light as upper air!

THOMAS HARDY

THE MOON AND THE SUN

DAISIES

The stars are everywhere to-night,
Above, beneath me and around;
They fill the sky with powdery light
And glimmer from the night-strewn ground;
For where the folded daisies are
In every one I see a star.

And so I know that when I pass
Where no sun's shadow counts the hours
And where the sky was there is grass
And where the stars were there are flowers,
Through the long night in which I lie
Stars will be shining in my sky.

ANDREW YOUNG

THE HORSEMAN

I heard a horseman
    Ride over the hill;
The moon shone clear,
    The night was still;
His helm was silver,
    And pale was he;
And the horse he rode
    Was of ivory.

WALTER DE LA MARE

STAR-TALK

"Are you awake, Gemelli,
    This frosty night?"
"We'll be awake till reveille,
Which is Sunrise," say the Gemelli,
"It's no good trying to go to sleep:
If there's wine to be got we'll drink it deep,
    But sleep is gone for tonight,
    But sleep is gone for tonight."

"Are you cold too, poor Pleiads,
    This frosty night?"

"Yes, and so are the Hyads:
See us cuddle and hug," say the Pleiads,
"All six in a ring: it keeps us warm:
We huddle together like birds in a storm:
    It's bitter weather tonight,
    It's bitter weather tonight."

"What do you hunt, Orion,
    This starry night?"
"The Ram, the Bull and the Lion,
And the Great Bear," says Orion,
"With my starry quiver and beautiful belt
I am trying to find a good thick pelt
    To warm my shoulders tonight,
    To warm my shoulders tonight."

"Did you hear that, Great She-bear,
    This frosty night?"
"Yes, he's talking of stripping *me* bare,
Of my own big fur," says the She-bear.
"I'm afraid of the man and his terrible arrow:
The thought of it chills my bones to the marrow,
    And the frost so cruel tonight!
    And the frost so cruel tonight!"

"How is your trade, Aquarius,
    This frosty night?"
"Complaints is many and various,
And my feet are cold," says Aquarius,

"There's Venus objects to the Dolphin-scales,
And Mars to Crab-spawn found in my pails,
   And the pump has frozen tonight,
   And the pump has frozen tonight."

ROBERT GRAVES

RIDDLE #29: THE MOON AND THE SUN

I saw a silvery creature scurrying
Home, as lovely and light as heaven
Itself, running with stolen treasure
Between its horns. It hoped, by deceit
And daring and art, to set an arbor
There in that soaring castle. Then,
A shining creature, known to everyone
On earth, climbed the mountains and cliffs,
Rescued his prize, and drove the wily
Impostor back to darkness. It fled
To the west, swearing revenge. The morning
Dust scattered away, dew
Fell, and the night was gone. And no one
Knew where the soft-footed thief had vanished.

translated from the Old English
by BURTON RAFFEL

THE CAT AND THE MOON

The cat went here and there
And the moon spun round like a top,
And the nearest kin of the moon,
The creeping cat, looked up.
Black Minnaloushe stared at the moon,
For, wander and wail as he would,
The pure cold light in the sky
Troubled his animal blood.
Minnaloushe runs in the grass
Lifting his delicate feet.
Do you dance, Minnaloushe, do you dance?
When two close kindred meet,
What better than call a dance?
Maybe the moon may learn,
Tired of that courtly fashion,
A new dance turn.
Minnaloushe creeps through the grass
From moonlit place to place,
The sacred moon overhead
Has taken a new phase.
Does Minnaloushe know that his pupils
Will pass from change to change,
And that from round to crescent,
From crescent to round they range?

Minnaloushe creeps through the grass
Alone, important and wise,
And lifts to the changing moon
His changing eyes.

W. B. YEATS

YEAR'S END

SPRING AND FALL:
TO A YOUNG CHILD

Márgarét, are you gríeving
Over Goldengrove unleaving?
Leáves, líke the things of man, you
With your fresh thoughts care for, can you?
Áh! ás the heart grows older
It will come to such sights colder
By and by, nor spare a sigh
Though worlds of wanwood leafmeal lie;
And yet you wíll weep and know why.
Now no matter, child, the name:
Sórrow's spríngs áre the same.
Nor mouth had, no nor mind, expressed
What heart heard of, ghost guessed:
It ís the blight man was born for,
It is Margaret you mourn for.

GERARD MANLEY HOPKINS

SEPTEMBER

The goldenrod is yellow,
    The corn is turning brown,
The trees in apple orchards
    With fruit are bending down.

The gentian's bluest fringes
    Are curling in the sun;
In dusty pods the milkweed
    Its hidden silk has spun;

The sedges flaunt their harvest
    In every meadow nook,
And asters by the brookside
    Make asters in the brook;

From dewy lanes at morning
    The grapes' sweet odors rise;
At noon the roads all flutter
    With yellow butterflies—

By all these lovely tokens
    September days are here,
With summer's best of weather
    And autumn's best of cheer.

        HELEN HUNT JACKSON

OCTOBER

O hushed October morning mild,
Thy leaves have ripened to the fall;
Tomorrow's wind, if it be wild,
Should waste them all.
The crows above the forest call;
Tomorrow they may form and go.
O hushed October morning mild,
Begin the hours of this day slow.
Make the day seem to us less brief.
Hearts not averse to being beguiled,
Beguile us in the way you know.
Release one leaf at break of day;
At noon release another leaf;
One from our trees, one far away.
Retard the sun with gentle mist;
Enchant the land with amethyst.
Slow, slow!
For the grapes' sake, if they were all,
Whose leaves already are burnt with frost,
Whose clustered fruit must else be lost—
For the grapes' sake along the wall.

ROBERT FROST

WHEN ICICLES HANG BY THE WALL

When icicles hang by the wall
    And Dick the shepherd blows his nail
And Tom bears logs into the hall
    And milk comes frozen home in pail,
When blood is nipp'd and ways be foul,
Then nightly sings the staring owl,
              Tu-whit tu-who;
A merry note,
While greasy Joan doth keel the pot.

When all aloud the wind doth blow
    And coughing drowns the parson's saw
And birds sit brooding in the snow
    And Marian's nose looks red and raw,
When roasted crabs hiss in the bowl,
Then nightly sings the staring owl,
              Tu-whit tu-who;
A merry note
While greasy Joan doth keel the pot.

WILLIAM SHAKESPEARE

SONG

Lovely hill-torrents are
    At cold winterfall;
Among the earth's silence, they
    Stonily call.

Gone Autumn's pageantry;
    Through woods all bare
With strange, locked voices
    Shining they stare!

W. J. TURNER

LANDSCAPE, DEER SEASON

Snorting his pleasure in the dying sun,
The buck surveys his commodious estate,
Not sighting the red nostrils of the gun
Until too late.

He is alone. His body holds stock-still,
Then like a monument it falls to earth;
While the blood-red target-sun, over our hill,
Topples to death.

BARBARA HOWES

SNOW IN THE SUBURBS

Every branch big with it,
Bent every twig with it;
Every fork like a white web-foot;
Every street and pavement mute:
Some flakes have lost their way, and grope back upward, when
Meeting those meandering down they turn and descend again,
The palings are glued together like a wall,
And there is no waft of wind with the fleecy fall.

A sparrow enters the tree
Whereon immediately
A snow-lump thrice his own slight size
Descends on him and showers his head and eyes.
And overturns him,
And near inurns him,
And lights on a nether twig, when its brush
Starts off a volley of other lodging lumps with a rush.

The steps are a blanched slope,
Up which, with feeble hope,
A black cat comes, wide-eyed and thin;
And we take him in.

THOMAS HARDY

VELVET SHOES

Let us walk in the white snow
    In a soundless space;
With footsteps quiet and slow,
    At a tranquil pace,
    Under veils of white lace.

I shall go shod in silk,
    And you in wool,
White as a white cow's milk,
    More beautiful
    Than the breast of a gull.

We shall walk through the still town
    In a windless peace;
We shall step upon white down,
    Upon silver fleece,
    Upon softer than these.

We shall walk in velvet shoes:
    Wherever we go
Silence will fall like dews
    On white silence below.
    We shall walk in the snow.

ELINOR WYLIE

A CHRISTMAS CAROLL, SUNG TO THE KING IN THE PRESENCE AT WHITE-HALL

Chor.   What sweeter musick can we bring,
        Then a Caroll, for to sing
        The Birth of this our heavenly King?
        Awake the Voice! Awake the String!
        Heart, Eare, and Eye, and every thing
        Awake! the while the active Finger
        Runs division with the Singer

FROM THE FLOURISH THEY CAME TO THE SONG

1   Dark and dull night, flie hence away,
    And give the honour to this Day,
    That sees *December* turn'd to *May*,

2   If we may ask the reason, say;
    The why, and wherefore all things here
    Seem like the Spring-time of the yeere?

3   Why do's the chilling Winters morne
    Smile, like a field beset with corne?
    Or smell, like to a Meade new-shorne,
    Thus, on the sudden? 4. Come and see
    The cause, why things thus fragrant be:
    'Tis He is borne, whose quickning Birth
    Gives life and luster, publike mirth,
    To Heaven, and the under-Earth.

Chor.   We see Him come, and know Him ours,
         Who, with His Sun-shine, and His showers
         Turnes all the patient ground to flowers.

   1   The Darling of the world is come,
         And fit it is, we finde a roome
         To welcome Him. 2. The nobler part
         Of all the house here, is the heart,

Chor.   Which we will give Him; and bequeath
         This Hollie, and this Ivie Wreath,
         To do Him honour; who's our King,
         And Lord of all this Revelling.

The Musicall Part was composed by M. Henry Lawes.

ROBERT HERRICK

STOPPING BY WOODS ON A SNOWY EVENING

Whose woods these are I think I know.
His house is in the village though;
He will not see me stopping here
To watch his woods fill up with snow.

My little horse must think it queer
To stop without a farmhouse near
Between the woods and frozen lake
The darkest evening of the year.

He gives his harness bells a shake
To ask if there is some mistake.
The only other sound's the sweep
Of easy wind and downy flake.

The woods are lovely, dark and deep,
But I have promises to keep,
And miles to go before I sleep,
And miles to go before I sleep.

ROBERT FROST

AUTHOR INDEX

Adams, Léonie *(1899–)*	
Country Summer	98
Song from a Country Fair	234
Aiken, Conrad *(1889–)*	
Portrait of a Girl	123
Auden, W. H. *(1907–)*	
Their Lonely Betters	87
Austin, Mary *(1868–1934)*	
Grizzly Bear	4
Beddoes, Thomas Lovell *(1803–1849)*	
The Mighty Thoughts of an Old World	201
Belloc, Hilaire *(1870–1953)*	
The Frog	10
Sarah Byng Who Could Not Read and Was Tossed into a Thorny Hedge by a Bull	112
Bishop, Elizabeth *(1911–)*	
The Fish	67
Bishop, John Peale *(1891–1944)*	
The Birds of Paradise	67
Blake, William *(1757–1827)*	
The Blossom	97
Infant Joy	132
Introduction	131
The Lamb	64
Laughing Song	41
Blunden, Edmund *(1896–)*	
The Midnight Skaters	235
Bogan, Louise *(1897–)*	
M., Singing	137
Musician	132
Bridges, Robert *(1844–1930)*	
I Have Loved Flowers	83

Browning, Robert *(1812–1889)*
  Pippa's Song — 96
Campion, Thomas *(1567–1620)*
  There Is a Garden in Her Face — 125
Carroll, Lewis *(1832–1898)*
  Father William — 154
  Jabberwocky — 148
Causley, Charles *(1917–   )*
  Nursery Rhyme of Innocence and Experience — 170
Chesterton, G. K. *(1874–1936)*
  The Song of Quoodle — 107
Clare, John *(1793–1864)*
  The Thrush's Nest — 91
Cole, William *(1919–   )*
  Just Dropped In — 153
Coleridge, Samuel Taylor *(1772–1834)*
  Kubla Khan — 222
Collymore, Frank A. *(1893–   )*
  The Zobo Bird — 156
Colum, Padraic *(1881–   )*
  Condors — 75
  Dahlias — 81
  I Saw the Wind Today — 34
Cornford, Frances *(1886–1960)*
  To a Fat Lady Seen from the Train — 106
Cummings, E. E. *(1894–1962)*
  All in Green Went My Love Riding — 121
de la Mare, Walter *(1873–1956)*
  All That's Past — 202
  The Barber's — 25
  Bunches of Grapes — 23
  Gone — 205
  The Horseman — 242
  Miss. T. — 22
  The Song of the Mad Prince — 136
Dickinson, Emily *(1830–1886)*
  A Bird Came Down the Walk — 77

A Narrow Fellow in the Grass	65
Success Is Counted Sweetest	191
There Is No Frigate Like a Book	218
Dinesen, Isak *(1885–1963)*	
Zebra	88
Drinkwater, John *(1882–1937)*	
Snail	85
Eliot, T. S. *(1888–1964)*	
Cape Ann	53
Emerson, Ralph Waldo *(1803–1882)*	
The Mountain and the Squirrel	26
Field, Eugene *(1850–1895)*	
The Sioux	154
Fitzgerald, F. Scott *(1896–1940)*	
There'd Be an Orchestra	135
Flecker, James Elroy *(1884–1915)*	
The Golden Journey to Samarkand (Prologue)	228
Santorin	183
Stillness	126
Francis, Robert *(1901–)*	
The Base Stealer	212
Frost, Robert *(1875–1963)*	
The Last Word of a Bluebird	13
October	251
The Pasture	44
The Runaway	72
Stopping by Woods on a Snowy Evening	257
Grahame, Kenneth *(1859–1931)*	
Duck's Ditty	50
The Song of Mr. Toad	108
Graves, Robert *(1895–)*	
Allie	81
Henry and Mary	10
The Six Badgers	76
Star-Talk	242
Greenaway, Kate *(1846–1901)*	
Little Wind	33

Hardy, Thomas *(1840–1928)*
   The Garden Seat   237
   The Roman Road   200
   Snow in the Suburbs   254
H. D. [Hilda Doolittle] *(1886–1961)*
   Oread   177
Herrick, Robert *(1591–1674)*
   Another Grace for a Child   29
   A Christmas Caroll, Sung to the King in the Presence at White-Hall   256
   His Cavalier   109
   His Grange, or Private Wealth   21
   A Ternarie of Littles, upon a Pipkin of Jellie Sent to a Lady   24
   To Daffadills   70
   To Musique, To Becalme His Fever   133
Hodgson, Ralph *(1871–1962)*
   The Bells of Heaven   20
   The Hammers   202
   A Song   127
   A Wood Song   96
Hoffmann, Heinrich *(1809–1894)*
   The Story of Augustus Who Would Not Have Any Soup   114
Hopkins, Gerard Manley *(1844–1889)*
   Pied Beauty   47
   Spring and Fall: To a Young Child   249
Housman, Alfred Edward *(1859–1936)*
   Into My Heart   199
Howes, Barbara *(1914–   )*
   Early Supper   27
   Landscape, Deer Season   253
Jackson, Helen Hunt *(1830–1885)*
   September   250
Keats, John *(1795–1821)*
   La Belle Dame Sans Merci   163
Kelly, Walt *(1913–   )*
   Boston Charlie   152

Kennedy, X. J. *(1929–)*
   Little Elegy — 234
Kinnell, Galway *(1927–)*
   First Song — 47
Kipling, Rudyard *(1865–1936)*
   Cities and Thrones and Powers — 197
Landor, Walter Savage *(1775–1864)*
   On Music — 140
Lawrence, D. H. *(1885–1930)*
   Bavarian Gentians — 84
Lear, Edward *(1812–1888)*
   Cold Are the Crabs — 39
   The Jumblies — 145
   Limericks — 9
   The Owl and the Pussy Cat — 14
   Teapots and Quails — 5
Lindsay, Vachel *(1879–1931)*
   The Flower-fed Buffaloes — 203
   The Little Turtle — 79
   The Mysterious Cat — 88
Lofting, Hugh *(1886–1947)*
   Picnic — 4
Longfellow, Henry Wadsworth *(1807–1882)*
   My Lost Youth — 178
Macdonald, George *(1824–1905)*
   The Wind and the Moon — 35
MacLeish, Archibald *(1892–)*
   The Too-Late Born — 192
Manifold, John *(1915–)*
   Fife Tune — 193
McCord, David *(1897–)*
   Tiger Lily — 74
Meynell, Alice *(1847–1922)*
   The Rainy Summer — 99
Millay, Edna St. Vincent *(1892–1950)*
   Counting-out Rhyme — 7
   Look, Edwin! — 115

Miller, Vassar *(1924–   )*
  At a Child's Baptism ... 28
Milne, A. A. *(1882–1956)*
  The Three Foxes ... 12
Monro, Harold *(1879–1932)*
  Overheard on a Saltmarsh ... 227
Moore, Marianne *(1887–   )*
  A Talisman ... 199
Nash, Odgen *(1902–   )*
  The Purist ... 111
Poe, Edgar Allen *(1809–1849)*
  The Raven ... 165
Potter, Beatrix *(1866–1943)*
  The Old Woman ... 8
Pound, Ezra *(1885–   )*
  An Immorality ... 119
Raffel, Burton [translator] *(1928–   )*
  Riddle #29: The Moon and the Sun ... 244
Reed, Henry *(1914–   )*
  Naming of Parts ... 189
Reese, Lizette Woodworth *(1856–1935)*
  Lydia Is Gone This Many a Year ... 236
Richards, Laura *(1850–1943)*
  Eletelephony ... 7
Roberts, Elizabeth Madox *(1885–1941)*
  The Butterbean Tent ... 48
  The Cornfield ... 46
  Firefly—a Song ... 78
  The Hens ... 51
  Milking Time ... 45
  The People ... 105
Robinson, Edwin Arlington *(1869–1935)*
  The Dark Hills ... 189
  The House on the Hill ... 204
Roethke, Theodore *(1908–1963)*
  The Bat ... 80
  Big Wind ... 213
  The Lady and the Bear ... 151

Rossetti, Christina *(1830–1894)*
    The Caterpillar — 90
    Ferry Me across the Water — 11
    The Horses of the Sea — 42
    Minnie and Mattie — 40
    What Is Pink? — 3
    Who Has Seen the Wind? — 33

Scott, Winfield Townley *(1916–   )*
    Landscape as Metal and Flowers — 209

Shakespeare, William *(1564–1616)*
    Ariel's Dirge — 141
    Ariel's Song — 138
    Song from Twelfth Night, Act II, Scene 3 — 140
    When Icicles Hang by the Wall — 252

Shapiro, Karl *(1913–   )*
    Manhole Covers — 214

Skelton, John *(1460?–1529)*
    To Mistress Margaret Hussey — 109

Smith, William Jay *(1918–   )*
    Butterfly — 92
    Dog — 90
    A Pavane for the Nursery — 124

Spender, Stephen *(1909–   )*
    The Express — 210

Stephens, James *(1882–1950)*
    The Goat Paths — 56
    Little Things — 19

Stevens, Wallace *(1879–1955)*
    Earthy Anecdote — 225
    Ploughing on Sunday — 52
    The Snow Man — 226

Stevenson, Robert Louis *(1850–1894)*
    Bed in Summer — 100
    Foreign Children — 105
    Rain — 34
    The Swing — 25
    Where Go the Boats — 177
    Windy Nights — 35

Swinburne, Algernon Charles *(1837–1909)*
   Envoi — 79
Tagore, Rabindranath *(1861–1941)*
   The Home — xix
Tennyson, Alfred, Lord *(1809–1892)*
   Break, Break, Break — 182
   The Brook — 42
   The Eagle — 74
   See What a Lovely Shell — 185
   Song—The Owl — 73
   The Splendor Falls on Castle Walls — 139
Thomas, Dylan *(1914–1953)*
   Fern Hill — 53
   Johnnie Crack and Flossie Snail — 150
Thomas, Edward *(1878–1917)*
   Adlestrop — 86
   If I Should Ever by Chance — 20
   Will You Come? — 120
Turner, W. J. *(1889–1946)*
   Romance — 220
   Song — 253
Untermeyer, Louis *(1885–   )*
   At the Bottom of the Well — 218
Walcott, Derek *(1930–   )*
   Alba — 212
Waller, Edmund *(1606–1687)*
   Song — 128
Wilbur, Richard *(1921–   )*
   Digging for China — 224
Williams, William Carlos *(1883–1963)*
   The Dance — 137
   Flowers by the Sea — 86
   This Is Just to Say — 211
Wilson, Edmund *(1895–   )*
   Peterhof — 153
Wolfe, Humbert *(1885–1940)*
   The Blackbird — 75
   The Gray Squirrel — 65

Wordsworth, William *(1770–1850)*
    Daffodils 71
    Written in March 95
Wright, Judith *(1915–)*
    Egrets 63
    Lyrebirds 217
Wylie, Elinor *(1885–1928)*
    Velvet Shoes 255
Yeats, William Butler *(1865–1939)*
    The Cat and the Moon 245
    An Irish Airman Foresees His Death 191
    The Old Men Admiring Themselves in the Water 198
    The Song of Wandering Aengus 142
    When You Are Old 233
    Who Goes with Fergus? 135
Young, Andrew *(1885–)*
    Daisies 241
    The Old Tree 49
Anonymous
    Riddle #29: The Moon and the Sun 244
    Sir Patrick Spens 159

TITLE INDEX

Adlestrop, THOMAS, E. 86
Alba, WALCOTT 212
All in Green Went My Love Riding, CUMMINGS 121
All That's Past, DE LA MARE 202
Allie, GRAVES 81
Another Grace for a Child, HERRICK 29
Ariel's Dirge, SHAKESPEARE 141
Ariel's Song, SHAKESPEARE 138
At a Child's Baptism, MILLER 28
At the Bottom of the Well, UNTERMEYER 218

Barber's, The, DE LA MARE	25
Base Stealer, The, FRANCIS	212
Bat, The, ROETHKE	80
Bavarian Gentians, LAWRENCE	84
Bed in Summer, STEVENSON	100
Belle Dame Sans Merci, La, KEATS	163
Bells of Heaven, The, HODGSON	20
Big Wind, ROETHKE	213
Bird Came Down the Walk, A, DICKINSON	77
Birds of Paradise, The, BISHOP, J. P.	67
Blackbird, The, WOLFE	75
Blossom, The, BLAKE	97
Boston Charlie, KELLY	152
Break, Break, Break, TENNYSON	182
Brook, The, TENNYSON	42
Bunches of Grapes, DE LA MARE	23
Butterbean Tent, The, ROBERTS	48
Butterfly, SMITH	92
Cape Ann, ELIOT	53
Cat and the Moon, The, YEATS	245
Caterpillar, The, ROSSETTI	90
Christmas Caroll, Sung to the King, A., HERRICK	256
Cities and Thrones and Powers, KIPLING	197
Cold Are the Crabs, LEAR	39
Condors, COLUM	75
Cornfield, The, ROBERTS	46
Counting-out Rhyme, MILLAY	7
Country Summer, ADAMS	98
Daffodils, WORDSWORTH	71
Dahlias, COLUM	81
Daisies, YOUNG	241
Dance, The, WILLIAMS	137
Dark Hills, The, ROBINSON	189
Digging for China, WILBUR	224
Dog, SMITH	90
Duck's Ditty, GRAHAME	50

Eagle, The, TENNYSON	74
Early Supper, HOWES	27
Earthy Anecdote, STEVENS	225
Egrets, WRIGHT	63
Eletelephony, RICHARDS	7
Envoi, SWINBURNE	79
Express, The, SPENDER	210
Father William, CARROLL	154
Fern Hill, THOMAS, D.	53
Ferry Me across the Water, ROSSETTI	11
Fife Tune, MANIFOLD	193
Firefly, ROBERTS	78
First Song, KINNELL	47
Fish, The, BISHOP, E.	67
Flower-fed Buffaloes, The, LINDSAY	203
Flowers by the Sea, WILLIAMS	86
Foreign Children, STEVENSON	105
Frog, The, BELLOC	10
Garden Seat, The, HARDY	237
Goat Paths, The, STEPHENS	56
Golden Journey to Samarkand, The (Prologue), FLECKER	228
Gone, DE LA MARE	205
Gray Squirrel, The, WOLFE	65
Grizzly Bear, AUSTIN	4
Hammers, The, HODGSON	202
Henry and Mary, GRAVES	10
Hens, The, ROBERTS	51
His Cavalier, HERRICK	109
His Grange, or Private Wealth, HERRICK	21
Home, The, TAGORE	xix
Horseman, The, DE LA MARE	242
Horses of the Sea, The, ROSSETTI	42
House on the Hill, The, ROBINSON	204

I Have Loved Flowers, BRIDGES	83
I Saw the Wind Today, COLUM	34
If I Should Ever by Chance, THOMAS, E.	20
Immorality, An, POUND	119
Infant Joy, BLAKE	132
Into My Heart, HOUSMAN	199
Introduction, BLAKE	131
Irish Airman Foresees His Death, An, YEATS	191
Jabberwocky, CARROLL	148
Johnnie Crack and Flossie Snail, THOMAS, D.	150
Jumblies, The, LEAR	145
Just Dropped In, COLE	153
Kubla Khan, COLERIDGE	222
Lady and the Bear, The, ROETHKE	151
Lamb, The, BLAKE	64
Landscape as Metal and Flowers, SCOTT	209
Landscape, Deer Season, HOWES	253
Last Word of a Bluebird, The, FROST	13
Laughing Song, BLAKE	41
Limericks, LEAR	9
Little Elegy, KENNEDY	234
Little Things, STEPHENS	19
Little Turtle, The, LINDSAY	79
Little Wind, GREENAWAY	33
Look, Edwin! MILLAY	115
Lydia Is Gone This Many a Year, REESE	236
Lyrebirds, WRIGHT	217
Manhole Covers, SHAPIRO	214
M., Singing, BOGAN	137
Midnight Skaters, The, BLUNDEN	235
Mighty Thoughts of an Old World, The, BEDDOES	201
Milking Time, ROBERTS	45
Minnie and Mattie, ROSSETTI	40
Miss T., DE LA MARE	22
Mountain and the Squirrel, The, EMERSON	26

Musician, BOGAN	132
My Lost Youth, LONGFELLOW	178
Mysterious Cat, The, LINDSAY	88
Naming of Parts, REED	189
Narrow Fellow in the Grass, A, DICKINSON	65
Nursery Rhyme of Innocence and Experience, CAUSLEY	170
October, FROST	251
Old Men Admiring Themselves in the Water, The, YEATS	198
Old Tree, The, YOUNG	49
Old Woman, The, POTTER	8
On Music, LANDOR	140
Oread, H.D.	177
Overheard on a Saltmarsh, MONRO	227
Owl and the Pussy Cat, The, LEAR	14
Pasture, The, FROST	44
Pavane for the Nursery, A, SMITH	124
People, The, ROBERTS	105
Peterhof, WILSON	153
Picnic, LOFTING	4
Pied Beauty, HOPKINS	47
Pippa's Song, BROWNING	96
Ploughing on Sunday, STEVENS	52
Portrait of a Girl, AIKEN	123
Purist, The, NASH	111
Rain, STEVENSON	34
Rainy Summer, The, MEYNELL	99
Raven, The, POE	165
Riddle #29: The Moon and the Sun, RAFFEL, translator	244
Roman Road, The, HARDY	200
Romance, TURNER	220
Runaway, The, FROST	72
Santorin, FLECKER	183
Sarah Byng Who Could Not Read, BELLOC	112

See What a Lovely Shell, TENNYSON	185
September, JACKSON	250
Sioux, The, FIELD	154
Sir Patrick Spens, ANONYMOUS	159
Six Badgers, The, GRAVES	76
Snail, DRINKWATER	85
Snow in the Suburbs, HARDY	254
Snow Man, The, STEVENS	226
Song, TURNER	253
Song, WALLER	128
Song, A, HODGSON	127
Song from a Country Fair, ADAMS	234
Song from Twelfth Night, SHAKESPEARE	140
Song of Mr. Toad, The, GRAHAME	108
Song of Quoodle, The, CHESTERTON	107
Song of the Mad Prince, The, DE LA MARE	136
Song of Wandering Aengus, The, YEATS	142
Song—The Owl, TENNYSON	73
Splendor Falls on Castle Walls, The, TENNYSON	139
Spring and Fall: To a Young Child, HOPKINS	249
Star-Talk, GRAVES	242
Stillness, FLECKER	126
Stopping by Woods on a Snowy Evening, FROST	257
Story of Augustus Who Would Not Have Any Soup, The, HOFFMANN	114
Success is Counted Sweetest, DICKINSON	191
Swing, The, STEVENSON	25
Talisman, A, MOORE	199
Teapots and Quails, LEAR	5
Ternarie of Littles, A, HERRICK	24
Their Lonely Betters, AUDEN	87
There Is a Garden in Her Face, CAMPION	125
There Is No Frigate Like a Book, DICKINSON	218
There'd Be an Orchestra, FITZGERALD	135
This Is Just to Say, WILLIAMS	211
Three Foxes, The, MILNE	12
Thrush's Nest, The, CLARE	91

Tiger Lily, MCCORD	74
To a Fat Lady Seen from the Train, CORNFORD	106
To Daffadills, HERRICK	70
To Mistress Margaret Hussey, SKELTON	109
To Musique, To Becalme His Fever, HERRICK	133
Too-Late Born, The, MACLEISH	192
Velvet Shoes, WYLIE	255
What Is Pink?, ROSSETTI	3
When Icicles Hang by the Wall, SHAKESPEARE	252
When You Are Old, YEATS	233
Where Go the Boats, STEVENSON	177
Who Goes with Fergus?, YEATS	135
Who Has Seen the Wind?, ROSSETTI	33
Will You Come?, THOMAS, E.	120
Wind and the Moon, The, MACDONALD	35
Windy Nights, STEVENSON	35
Wood Song, A, HODGSON	96
Written in March, WORDSWORTH	95
Zebra, DINESEN	88
Zobo Bird, The, COLLYMORE	156

THE GOLDEN JOURNEY *was set in Monticello, a Linotype revival of the Binny & Ronaldson Roman No. 1, cast originally in 1796, in Philadelphia. Monticello is a transitional type face similar in character to Baskerville and even more so to Bell.*

The illustrations were cut on imported pear wood by FRITZ KREDEL. *The edition was designed by* GEORGE SALTER.